Doing Ethical Rese

Doing Ethical Research

HANNAH FARRIMOND

First published 2013 by
PALGRAVE MACMILLAN

Palgrave Macmillan in the UK is an imprint of Macmillan Publishers Limited, registered in England, company number 785998, of Houndmills, Basingstoke, Hampshire RG21 6XS.

Palgrave Macmillan in the US is a division of St Martin's Press LLC, 175 Fifth Avenue, New York, NY 10010.

Palgrave Macmillan is the global academic imprint of the above companies and has companies and representatives throughout the world.

Palgrave® and Macmillan® are registered trademarks in the United States, the United Kingdom, Europe and other countries.

ISBN: 978–0–230–29747–0

This book is printed on paper suitable for recycling and made from fully managed and sustained forest sources. Logging, pulping and manufacturing processes are expected to conform to the environmental regulations of the country of origin.

A catalogue record for this book is available from the British Library.

A catalog record for this book is available from the Library of Congress.

10 9 8 7 6 5 4 3 2 1
22 21 20 19 18 17 16 15 14 13

Printed in China

To Petar, Lucia, Sophia and my mum.

Contents

Figures

Ethical Dilemmas

Acknowledgements

The support of the Economic and Social Research Council (ESRC) is gratefully acknowledged. The work was part of the programme of the ESRC Centre for Genomics in Society (EGENIS) at the University of Exeter, UK.

Introduction

*At five o'clock in the evening, Christina Maslach, a recently grad-
uated PhD, packed up her bags and went to meet her boyfriend,
Philip Zimbardo, who was working in the Social Psychology lab at
Stanford University. What she saw when she got there shocked her
deeply. One group of students, designated 'mock prisoners', wear-
ing bags on their heads and chains around their legs, were moving
to the toilet block accompanied by an aggressively shouting 'mock
guard'. Earlier, prisoners were physically assaulted by the guards
using their batons, to supposedly signify 'symbolic' power. Prisoner
416 later reported, 'I don't regard it as an experiment or a simu-
lation. It was a prison run by psychologists instead of run by the
state' (Zimbardo, Maslach, & Haney, 1999, p.19).*

*Over 100 people had passed through the basement over the past
few days. She was the only one who saw this scene for the ethical
catastrophe that it had become. She reported her strong concerns
to the lead experimenter, Zimbardo. The Stanford prison experiment was closed down early, six days after it had begun.*

The Stanford prison experiment raises many interesting ethical
questions. It is not clear whether the experiment was intrinsically
unethical. The participants were all willing volunteers; there was
no coercion. Zimbardo suggested that it could be re-run again with
greater monitoring of participants (Zimbardo 1973). Furthermore,
similar scenarios in which volunteers are confined in a small space
structured to provoke confrontation and violence appear on our
TV screens as popular entertainment (e.g. *Big Brother* or *Cast-
away*). Indeed, the experiment has been recreated as a TV show
on the BBC (Haslam & Reicher, 2006; Reicher & Haslam, 2006;
Zimbardo, 2006). At the time, and for decades afterwards, it has
provoked debate about what should or shouldn't be done in the
name of social research.

Although most research does not become infamous from an
ethical perspective, this does not mean it is free from ethical
dilemma. Once you start thinking critically from a research ethics

perspective, your research may provoke a host of questions to address:

- You are running a small-scale life history interview study with only five participants. Two of them suddenly want to withdraw. What next?
- Your student friend asks if you can help them interpret their survey data. They send a file including names and addresses marked 'confidential'. Should you help?
- You want to do research with 14-year-olds about their sexuality. You are worried if you ask for parental permission, no one will take part. What should you do?
- You are required to fill in an ethics form for an Institutional Review Board (IRB) or ethics committee. All the sections, on confidentiality, anonymity and informed consent, seem quite standard. Is it wrong to copy and paste sections from the Internet?
- You are thinking of doing covert research, not initially telling participants your aims. Is this ethical?
- Does anyone really destroy their data after five years?

Sometimes as a researcher, you are confronted by more serious ethical issues, such as a participant revealing a serious crime or abuse, becoming very distressed or needing help or a colleague or fellow student stealing someone else's work. Furthermore, if ethical issues arise in your research, it can be very stressful if you feel a weight of moral responsibility and are unsure how to act. I spend several days as a junior researcher pondering whether to accept a particular job which seemed contrary to my own personal beliefs; it was an emotionally charged time (see case study in Chapter 4).

As someone who has chaired and sat as a representative on a social science ethics board/committee for several years, I am often asked what appears to be a simple question by students or staff: '*is my research ethical?*' What makes research ethics fascinating, but problematic, is that two people may not give the same answer. However, if you have a good knowledge of ethical principles, are familiar with the institutional procedures around ethics and the norms in your discipline, and have thought critically about it, it gives your ethical decision-making greater integrity. In most cases, you are not the first person to consider how to seek consent from children, or whether covert research is ethical. Learning about what others have done to ensure high ethical standards is a key starting point.

WHY DO YOU NEED A BOOK ON RESEARCH ETHICS?

Up until now, research ethics has often been covered by a brief chapter in research design textbooks. There are more specialist research ethics books for academic researchers, but they tend to be long on the whys and wherefores of research ethics theory, and short on practical detail. In the US, UK, Canada, Australia as well as other European countries, students and researchers are required to submit projects for formal ethical review. This is as much the case for undergraduate projects as multi-million-pound grant applications. Opting out of the research ethics process is simply not an option. However, many students and researchers say that although they realise research ethics is important, they are unsure how to navigate the procedures and, at times, question if these procedures have anything to do with 'being ethical'.

The title *Doing Ethical Research* reflects my own view that research ethics is a practice. It is something you do; it is the actions you take (or don't take) during your research, not just an abstract intellectual exercise. This book is designed to take you step-by-step through thinking about ethics throughout the time-line of a project or research study. After reading this book, you will be able to

- identify key ethical principles,
- incorporate ethical considerations into project design,
- think through ethical 'hot topics' such as anonymity and confidentiality, social justice, researching with children or Internet research,
- write and gain institutional ethical approval,
- manage ethical dilemmas when running your project and
- critically reflect on the role of research ethics.

The guiding principle of this book is that thinking about ethics is fundamental to good research design and practice. It is not something that can be added afterwards. Furthermore, good ethical research cannot be reduced to a set of 'right answers'. There is no one way to be ethical and people often disagree about specifics such as whether interviews should always be anonymous or whether oral or written consent is more appropriate. A key feature in this book is the inclusion of 'ethical dilemmas' based on typical (but not actual) real-life ethical scenarios. These dilemmas, some of which raise multiple and complex ethical issues, often have no clear answer. They are exercises to provoke the reader into thinking through a particular ethical issue; and different people may view the same scenario from quite different ethical perspectives.

There are also many controversies within research ethics around which a considerable academic literature has grown. Some debates have continued decades, such as how one ensures informed consent or whether covert research is ever justified. Newer debates include questioning who benefits from participatory approaches, or whether the Internet is a 'free-for-all' in terms of research data. At the heart of these debates is the issue of the power relationship between the researcher and the researched. As a member of a research institution (whether student or professor), the researcher is usually in a position of knowledge, experience and higher social status in comparison with the participants (although not always, for example, if interviewing elite groups). There has been a backlash against viewing people as 'vehicles' for data collection, rather than as participants who should also be involved and/or benefit from research; how to construct the nature of that involvement is one of the continuing debates.

There has also been a sustained critique of the formal ethical review system of IRBs and ethics committees, as well as increasing sociological examination of ethics practices. I cover these controversies and debates to foster critical thinking about them rather than simply complying with procedure.

Overall, this book is designed to help students and researchers apply ethical principles to their own research in a thoughtful and insightful way, both meeting their institutional requirements such as gaining ethical review and also helping develop an 'ethical sense', resulting in more ethically sound research.

WHO IS THIS BOOK FOR?

This book is written for undergraduates, postgraduates and researchers confronted with ethics forms and wondering what to write or ethical dilemmas and wondering what do next. At the undergraduate level, this book will be useful to those tackling research ethics in the context of small-scale research projects. It will be extremely useful to postgraduates (master's and PhD level) and early career researchers dealing with IRBs and ethics committees, designing projects with significant ethical dimensions, writing a grant proposal with an ethics section or doing a methods course. Supervisors will find it useful to give this book to students facing these challenges. I also hope expert researchers will get something out of it; working in collaborative teams, in a new topic area or dealing with an unexpected ethical 'crisis' in a seemingly unproblematic study, all of these benefit from the extra attention on research ethics this book is designed to provide.

This book focuses only on research with people. Researchers use different terms to describe those participating in research studies: 'human subjects', 'participants', 'respondents' or, depending on the method, 'interviewees', 'gatekeepers' or 'informants'. I usually use the term 'participants' as it carries less connotations of power than 'subject'; it is also relatively easy for those taking part to understand and use this term themselves.

This book does not cover the epistemological and philosophical basis of ethics in great detail. It also does not cover animal research, clinical trials or human tissue research, which have country-specific ethical and legal regulations, specified elsewhere.

THE STRUCTURE OF THIS BOOK

This book can be used in two ways. You can read it from the start, working through the chapters to give you a comprehensive and critical view of how to practice research ethics. Alternatively, if you need information on a specific topic or to fill in an ethics form section, you can turn to the relevant chapter or Hot Topic. It is important to note that institutions (universities, IRBs, disciplinary bodies) have their own ethics guidelines and codes, of which you should be aware. This book should be used in conjunction with them, to help you better understand their guidelines and as a resource for creating high-quality ethics proposals.

Figure 1.1 shows the structure of *Doing Ethical Research*. Part I of this book covers the 'Ethical Basics'. Chapter 1 explains why ethical review has become both a moral and institutional requirement. Chapter 2 covers the key 'ethical principles' (e.g. respect for persons, social justice) that underlie ethical practices, including how moral norms differ between cultures. Chapter 3 introduces the standard procedures of formal ethical review through IRBs and Research Ethics Committees (RECs) in the US, UK, Canada, Australia and in developing countries, as well as covering critiques of these systems.

Part II focuses on 'Ethics in Practice'. These three chapters take the reader through the main stages or 'life cycle' of a research project with an 'ethical spotlight'. Chapter 4 considers how

Part III Ethical "Hot Topics"	• Informed consent • Privacy, anonymity, confidentiality • Assessment of possible harm • Vulnerable groups/sensitive topics • Children and young people • Internet research ethics	Appendix Ethical Codes Guidelines Resources

Part II
Ethics in
Practice
	• Research design and ethics
	• Writing a successful ethics
	  proposal
	• Ethical dilemmas when
	  running the project	

Part I Ethical Basics	• Thinking critically about research ethics • Ethical principles and codes • Ethical procedures, institutions and norms	

Figure 1.1 The structure of *Doing Ethical Research*.

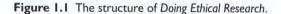

ethical thinking might inform research design in the first place. Chapter 5 looks specifically at how to create a good ethics proposal likely to gain approval from IRBs or RECs, with advice on how to avoid five common mistakes. Chapter 6 completes this section by considering how to handle ethical dilemmas that arise during the conduct of research, ranging from coping with participant distress to how to act if you become aware of potentially criminal acts or abuse.

Part III covers some key Hot Topics within research ethics: informed consent, PAC (privacy, anonymity and confidentiality), assessment of possible harms/risk to participants and researcher and research with children and vulnerable groups. For each topic, the reader is provided with information on why this is a perennial issue, including key theories and references, followed by realistic advice on how it can be addressed. A section on the particular ethical controversies of Internet research is also included.

The Appendix contains a selection of key codes, standards and guidelines in research ethics, plus useful websites.

Case studies are used throughout the book. Where they relate to my own work, I have used real examples. Others are composites or typical of cases I have come across having read over 200 social science ethics proposals over the past few years. No identifying details are given. Ethical 'horror stories' (cases which are infamous within research ethics) are included, but the emphasis is on providing realistic everyday examples of the type that researchers and students typically come across. The 'ethical dilemma' exercises contain questions to prompt discussion and debate. There are also 'quick questions' to provoke personal reflection on key issues.

MY PERSONAL TAKE ON RESEARCH ETHICS

My approach to ethics is not everyone's approach to ethics. Most IRBs or ethics committees operate relatively independently, and there is evidence that different committees may treat the same proposal differently (Angell, Sutton, Windridge, & Dixon-Woods, 2006; Redshaw, Harris, & Baum, 1996). Some may be mainly used to experimental or clinical paradigms and be unfamiliar with, for example, research in a very different culture or with qualitative methods. I consider my own approach to ethics to be rooted in researching in social science, aware of cultural differences, with a strong emphasis on researcher as well as participant well-being. Given that cultures around ethics review can vary between institutions and even departments in the same institution, you should check out your institutional requirements carefully before starting.

Part I
Ethical Basics

1 Thinking Critically about Research Ethics

WHY IS RESEARCH ETHICS IMPORTANT?

You cannot escape thinking about research ethics in social research these days (even if you wanted to!). It is now considered a key research skill to understand ethical principles, think about the ethics of your own research and undertake ethics review to meet institutional requirements. This was not always the case. When I was a psychology undergraduate in the UK, I used consent forms that were filled by my participants, but had little formal training in ethics, and very little understanding of *why* it was important to do so, or even why one might not want to use consent forms in some contexts.

This does not mean researchers and students in social research necessarily ignored ethical issues in the past. The ethics of the Stanford prison experiment discussed in the Introduction were highly controversial at the time (Zimbardo, 1973; Zimbardo et al., 1999). Another similarly controversial piece of research was Hoffman's 'Tearoom Trade' in 1970 (Hoffman, 1970; Humphries, 1970). This was a study of homosexual men who had sex with other men in public toilets (known as 'Tearooms'). He showed that many men who engaged in these practices had wives and families, thus breaking down many stereotypes about sexual orientation. However, the research method involved deception by tracking men home to interview them under false pretences, causing considerable disquiet within the research community (Humphries, 1970).

The difference between the past and now is the extent of the formalization of research practices. Research principles have become enshrined in disciplinary codes (e.g. the American Anthropological Association Code, the British Sociological Society Code) and institutionalized into processes, namely ethical review by Institutional Review Boards (IRBs) and Research

> **Quick question**
>
> *Imagine you agree to take part in a research project testing for a gene connected with hereditary heart disease. During the analysis, an 'unanticipated finding' comes up; you are positive for another gene related to early onset Alzheimer's disease. Would you want to know? Is there an ethical obligation for the doctors to tell you?*

Ethics Committees (RECs). Students undergo ethics training, or do projects about ethics. Ethical review is built into research timelines. Funding bodies demand it. Thinking about ethics is now a key skill in social research with human participants; this section tells you why it is important.

WHAT IS 'MORALITY' AND WHAT ARE 'RESEARCH ETHICS'?

The terms 'morality' or 'ethics' refers to what we believe to be 'right' and 'wrong' in terms of acceptable conduct (from a religious perspective, this may be referred to as 'good' and 'evil'). Much philosophical work has considered whether 'morals' and 'ethics' are the same thing; this book takes the practical view of Shamoo and Resnick (2009, p. 5) that most people use these terms interchangeably: to mean norms of conduct of what is acceptable and not acceptable. What is ethical is expressed in terms of first principles or values. These have a strong socially normative dimension, in other words, what everyone agrees is 'right' is often considered ethical. Ethical practice in social research involves consciously considering ethical values and making decisions based on them, variously referred to as 'ethical sensitivity', 'ethical awareness', or 'ethical mindfulness' (Guillemin, McDougall, & Gillam, 2009). Ethical codes and guidelines have been developed to express the core values, principles and procedures for a particular group (e.g. the Belmont Code for human participants, see Case Study in Chapter 2) or for disciplines (e.g. the American Psychological Association Code; American Psychological Association, 2002). Again, these are highly socially normative, and constitute what that professional group agrees are acceptable standards of conduct (e.g. the APA's 'Ethical Standards'). Equally codes can be imposed as a requirement on a group as much as being an expression of collective agreement (Hammersley, 2006). Ethical review is a set of regulatory practices which aim to promote ethical standards. These are governed not only by codes but, in the US, by federal law concerning human participant research. Ethical review is usually conducted by formal bodies such as IRBs or ethics committees. When we talk about 'research ethics', we refer to the ethical norms, codes and regulation which govern our current research practices as part of an academic/scientific professional community. It is important to note that much of the formal codification and standardization of research ethics developed in a particular historical context, primarily within biomedicine, as the result of ethical abuse and the mistreatment of human subjects (see Case Study in Chapter 2). The applicability of such medical models for social research has been brought into question (e.g. Lincoln & Tierney, 2004; Murphy & Dingwall, 2007) (see Chapter 3 for more on critiques of ethics review).

However, the existence of commonly agreed ethical principles and codes does not mean everyone always agrees upon what is ethical in a particular given scenario. Resnick has argued that the definition of an ethical dilemma is when one is confronted by two different actions, both supported by a basic ethical principle (Resnick, 1998). 'Applied ethics' is a branch of ethics concerned with applying ethical principles in practice, often in controversial situations. The problem of 'unanticipated findings' during medical testing, presented in the 'quick question' in this chapter, is just a case of such an applied dilemma. One person in the testing team might think it highly unethical to give any participant an additional finding, as they did not consent to be tested for other conditions and may actively not want to know the result. Another team member might argue that to withhold vital information about a serious condition could cause preventable harm to the participant. On this basis, it could be argued to be unethical not to tell them.

However, although two people may not agree on the ethical course of action, no one would argue that ethics do not matter in this situation. There is a 'moral or ethical obligation' to think and act. Doing research ethics in practice is not just about knowing formal codes and getting through review boards. Ethical practice is about what people think and do as part of their everyday research life, for example, in discussions between a student and supervisor about 'the right thing to do' when an ethical problem comes up in a study they are performing together, or in personal reflection when you wonder why you don't want to study certain topics as they seem intrinsically 'wrong', or in working with others to expose or change a social problem.

Morality is not the same as the law, although they often overlap. Legal rules are designed to enforce limits on behaviour. However, laws can be considered unethical. If you believe that abortion is morally wrong, then laws which allow abortion are unethical to you, even if they are legal. There are also laws which refer specifically to ethical research procedures. In the UK, the Mental Capacity Act (2005) sets out the legal standards of involvement in research for vulnerable adults, and in the US, federal regulations are legally binding on those conducting human participant research (45 CRF Part 46 of the Common Rule). It has been argued that procedures in ethical review (e.g. signing written consent forms) increasingly resemble legalistic contracts due to a culture in which institutions fear being prosecuted (e.g. Adler & Adler, 2002).

MORAL REASONS

The failure to act ethically in relation to human subjects can have severe consequences for them. The 'moral requirement' argument for research ethics is that it is important to act ethically in relation to your participants *above and beyond* any formal or procedural ethics requirements in your institution or organization.

There are several philosophical theories which give rise to ways of moral reasoning. I do not think you necessarily need to personally adopt a philosophical theory and stick with it to make ethical decisions in social research. Rather, knowing about these philosophical positions helps in understanding why, given the same scenario and the same core principles, researchers sometimes profoundly disagree on what is the ethical course of action.

Deontological

The Kantian position is that there is an intrinsic reason 'to do the right thing' in relation to universal moral principles and our duty to others. From this perspective, the moral imperative to follow principles such as respect for persons, doing no harm and social justice holds across any part of your life, not just in your research. Participants should not be just a means to obtain data or further knowledge. One way of judging what is 'right' is to consider what would happen if everyone followed the behaviour in question (the so-called Categorical Imperative). Whether something is ethical or not is the result of moral motives and following moral laws, not about their outcomes.

Many disciplinary ethics codes contain a list of moral principles, stated as imperatives e.g. 'do no harm'. One difficulty of such codes is that they are very decontextualized; it is difficult to know what moral behaviour might look like in different contexts. Furthermore, dilemmas arise where decision-makers all come from an equally moral motivation, but disagree about the application of these principles, as the 'unanticipated results' quick question shows.

Utilitarianism

Another strand of philosophical moral reasoning relates to the utility of outcomes. From a utilitarian perspective, ethical human subjects research can be evaluated against a cost–benefit analysis; does doing research in this way benefit the majority of people? Not all ethical codes subscribe to a utilitarian rationale. The Nuremberg Code developed after World War II (see Case Study in Chapter 2), for example, warns against prioritizing societal interests over that of any individual 'in research on man, the interest of science and society should never take precedence over considerations related to the well being of the subject'.

Utilitarian reasoning is often in evidence in debates about covert research, in which deception (a 'wrong') is used in the service of another principle (to increase social justice, to further knowledge). For example, Lenza has argued that the ethical problems of the Tearoom Trade study (described earlier in this chapter) have to be weighed against the ethical positives that stemmed from shattering myths about homosexual men, which went on to change both policy and legislation for the better (Lenza, 2004). However, it could also be argued that covert research (or, as Von Hoffman named

15

it at the time, 'snooping') damages the social research enterprise as a whole (Hoffman, 1970). Doing research holding high ethical standards does make sense from a utilitarian perspective, as it ensures a socially beneficial research culture in which funders and participants are motivated to participate.

VIRTUE ETHICS

This sense of ethics relates to having a moral character. Ethical behaviour is about living a life which is virtuous through practicing good traits, including honesty, truthfulness, courage, benevolence, being humble and so on.

Professional ethics codes (about the correct behaviour in one's profession) often refer to such virtues, particularly honesty and integrity. Breaches of these virtues include falsifying data, stealing someone else's ideas, or hiding conflicts of interest. Shamoo and Resnick argue that 'integrity' (having a morally consistent aspect that runs through our beliefs, actions and character) is a particularly important virtue in research ethics (2009, p. 14).

Another type of virtue ethics is the 'ethics of care' or 'relational ethics', which has developed through feminist critiques of ethics as a process of rational decision-making based on abstract principles (Gilligan, 1982; Held, 2005; Noddings, 1984). From this perspective, the emotional relationship between researcher and participant should be the primary focus of ethics. In particular there is an emphasis on the interdependency of humans, rather than their autonomy. This creates a moral obligation to care for dependent groups (older people, children), as well as to use emotional virtues (e.g. sensitivity, responsiveness, friendship) when interacting with people.

HUMAN RIGHTS THEORY

The human or 'natural' rights approach starts from the premise that participants are first and foremost humans, with a set of natural human rights (Shamoo & Resnick, 2009). These include the right to life, liberty, freedom of thought, religious freedom, freedom from persecution and equality. Rights are only restricted according to certain criteria, for example, if an action may cause harm. What constitutes 'harm' and a 'minimal risk' of harm in research ethics (and thus should restrict research) has been the subject of extensive debate, at both philosophical and practical levels (see Hot Topic 'Assessment of Possible Harm').

SOCIAL JUSTICE RESEARCH

In the past 20 years, there has been an increasing focus on research explicitly oriented around social justice, such as action, participatory and transformative research (Brydon-Miller, 2010; Lewin, 1946; Mertens, 2009). These approaches are not necessarily aligned to one philosophical theory, but share a common purpose: the promotion of social justice through social research. Action research (AR) has been used extensively in education, and to a lesser extent health care, with practitioners critically reflecting on their own workplace, to identify problems and formulate a plan, implement it and evaluate it, in a cyclical fashion of improvement (Greenwood & Levin, 1998). Participatory research has as its goal the structural transformation for the benefit of the less powerful (e.g. minorities, excluded groups) (Hall, 1981). Ennew and Beasley suggest that, at a practical level, two features of participatory research are (a) participants being involved in establishing the research questions and design and (b) participants collecting and analysing the data (Ennew & Beasley, 2006). The transformative paradigm is 'a framework of belief systems that directly engages members of culturally diverse groups with a focus on increased social justice' (Mertens, Holmes, & Harris, 2009, p. 86). Transformative approaches particularly focus on the resilience and capabilities that already exist within marginalized communities, rather than simply taking a 'problem-oriented' approach which focuses on their deficits.

Although these approaches are not identical, they represent a foregrounding of the 'ethical imperative' in research. From these perspectives, research becomes ethical through its purpose: to

17

encourage social change, emancipate, enlighten, challenge dominant groups and speak for the powerless. It is also an explicitly political agenda in which the researcher acts with others to promote change. These approaches have also been associated with a critique of 'top down' methods (such as in traditional positivistic research) which reinforce the hierarchical power relationship between the researcher and the researched. These approaches emphasize the need for a different (democratic) set of ethical practices, particularly concerning increased participant involvement, so that participants are treated as equal and are involved in collaborative research design.

It is now becoming standard to question in ethics review the extent of participant input and the participant benefits of a project, partly due to participatory/transformative agenda-setting in this area. However, such approaches are not an ethical panacea, nor claim to be (e.g. Williamson & Prosser, 2002). There can also be difficulties when gaining formal ethical review for participatory approaches (Boser, 2007; Khanlou & Peter, 2005) (also see Chapter 3).

MORAL REASONS FOR DOING ETHICAL RESEARCH

- *Participants are not a means to an end*: Ethical research treats participants as humans with intrinsic moral worth, and not just as a means of obtaining data or knowledge.
- *Research ethics are simply ethics*: The principles of research ethics, such as respect for people, doing no harm and social justice are important human values and rights in all spheres of life, not just research ethics.
- *Good research is ethical research*: Principles such as integrity and honesty promote the goals of good (valid) research (Resnick, 1998).
- *Ethical research has ethical outcomes*: The promotion of social justice or academic freedom is beneficial to society as a whole.
- *Caring about participants is an extension of our duty to care for others*, particularly those who are vulnerable, disempowered or disadvantaged.

- *Social justice research has the potential to enact social change* at a micro (e.g. action research in a school) or macro level (e.g. giving disempowered groups a political voice).

INSTITUTIONAL REASONS

Doing ethical research is not the same as writing ethics proposals for review. Guillemin and Gillam (2004) refer to the distinction in terms of 'procedural ethics' and 'ethics in practice'. It is now common for research institutions (e.g. universities, research centres, applied research settings such as health care systems, prisons) to have defined procedural requirements for ethical review. This varies between countries and the type of research conducted. The UK, US, Canada, Australia, New Zealand and Nordic countries have more formal procedures in place. Typically this involves 'anticipatory review': submitting a proposal of research in advance to an ethics group, committee or board which reviews it from an ethical perspective, making amendments where necessary. Certain types of social research, such as 'minimal risk' (where the risks are typical to those experienced in everyday life), may not be fully reviewed. Details of institutional procedures for ethical review are discussed in Chapter 3.

Submitting your research to ethics review and obtaining proof of this (e.g. in the form of a certificate) is not now just a matter of satisfying internal institutional requirements, but may be required by funders, publishers and examiners. There is, at this current historical point, considerable importance placed on complying with research ethics systems; it is neither a trivial issue nor one to be pushed to the back of the queue when planning a research project. For this reason, you need to find out in advance what is required for institutional ethical review for your specific work, assignment or larger project. It sounds obvious, but you can only comply with these requirements if you know about them. Every year, I speak with stressed students or staff who have failed to notice that their particular topic or type of research will require a full review or can't meet the deadlines for submission. Others start the process of ethical review, but fail to submit amendments or collect the certificate (and then ring up from another country asking for it to be faxed!)

Not taking procedural ethics seriously could put your research or qualification in jeopardy.

INSTITUTIONAL REASONS FOR DOING ETHICAL RESEARCH

- *Your institutions/organization requires it*: This may not only fulfil internal requirements, but also country-based legislative, funding body or national agency requirements for ethical review.
- *Requirement for publication*: Many major science, social science, business studies, law and humanities journals now require a sentence in the paper describing where and how ethical review was carried out. You are also often asked to check or fill a box when submitting the paper to say that you have complied with the ethical procedures within that country or institution.
- *Proof of approval*: Many countries and organizations require you to carry a certificate of ethical approval, which evidences institutional approval and your identity.
- *Compulsory part of obtaining a qualification*: Some institutions require you to have completed a course or module on research ethics before accepting and issuing your qualification. If you are doing a master's or PhD, you may be required to provide documentation of ethical approval (e.g. in the thesis appendices).

There are several points relating to ethical practice here. Firstly, getting an ethics certificate does not necessarily mean you are doing ethical research. Preparing for ethics review and gaining approval is simply one point in the ethical 'lifecycle' of your project. Ethical issues and dilemmas present themselves along the 'lifecycle', from initial topic choice, to how to ethically represent the views of participants, to ensuring dissemination produces ethical outcomes (e.g. academic knowledge, social justice). For more on the 'lifecycle approach' to ethics, see Part II. Secondly, as a system, ethics review is designed to produce more ethical research by enforcing ethical standards. However, it is possible for ethics systems to be unethical. For example, as Hammersley (2006) points out, they may have unanticipated consequences which have unethical outcomes, such as restricting academic freedom. They may also be motivated by values which are ethically debatable, such as institutional reputation. Critiques of ethics review systems are considered in more depth in Chapter 3.

Despite the critiques, however, I believe the reasons for conducting ethical review remain strong. Firstly, it is true that for experienced researchers, institutional ethical review can be a routine procedure. This is not necessarily the case for students and early career researchers who may be encountering the whole concept of research ethics, or a specific ethical dilemma, for the first time. Secondly, even experienced researchers may come across a new set of ethical or legal issues. I have helped senior staff confront difficult problems relating to terrorism legislation or historic sexual abuse that arose unexpectedly in their research. Thirdly, filling in an ethics proposal concentrates your mind at that time point on the issue of ethics in your research project, shining a spotlight on potential issues before you start. It allows you to initiate discussion with supervisors, other students and ethics officers about the field of ethics particular to your project. Fourthly, ethics review by boards and committees is ideally part of a package of practices relating to research ethics, ranging from formal review, through training, to informal conversations and musings. It may be true that in a business model of higher education with a high throughput of students, there is less time for informal ethics practices which are the result of research relationships between staff and students. This may be another reason why more formal methods of transmitting research ethics knowledge have come to dominate.

Ideally, institutional ethics review is a starting point for the discussion of research ethics throughout the 'lifecycle' of the research project, not an end in itself. Institutional ethical review can have an important function which goes beyond the bureaucratic.

PRACTICAL MORAL REASONS

There are also several other reasons why engaging with ethical issues have what I term 'practical moral' reasons. By this I mean that they relate to 'doing the right thing' in terms of their underlying morality, but they also give practical tangible benefits to the researcher, participants, the wider academic community and society at large. As such, they combine deontological and utilitarian arguments.

- *Opportunity to think through potential issues in advance*: This allows researchers to anticipate and prepare for potential ethical dilemmas, many of which are common within specific fields (e.g. working with children).
- *Have well-informed participants who are not harmed by taking part*: Having well-informed and fully consenting participants is not only ethical, but practical; participants who understand what the research is about are less likely to withdraw or complain.
- *Prioritize researcher safety*: This is an often neglected aspect of research ethics, but researcher safety can be considerably enhanced by forward planning.
- *Help you comply with data protection legislation*: Thinking about where and how to store data before you collect it will help you comply with your institution and legislative requirements.
- *Work together ethically with colleagues*: Much human subjects research is produced collaboratively in teams, or with students working together, including across different disciplines or organizations. Having an agreed professional ethical code to work from helps harmonize ethical thinking and practices to a common basic standard, even if disagreements occur (Shamoo & Resnick, 2009).
- *Societal level promotion of a research culture*: A high level of respect and protection for participants creates a climate in which being a participant in research is seen as a valuable social role, which in turn encourages participation. A belief in the integrity of research also promotes state/societal investment in research funding.

Again, many of these arguments rest on the assumption that research ethics practices make things more ethical. For example, if the social outcome of the research ethics practices were that less research beneficial to society took place, it would be less ethical. In practice, systems and processes rarely produce one outcome. It may be that the current focus on the bureaucratic side of ethical review inhibits a minority of research but the majority is conducted at a higher ethical standard with consequent benefits.

SUMMARY

The current focus on research ethics is a product of a particular historical context, as a reaction to ethical abuse and mistreatment of research subjects. It is also associated with an increasingly administrative/business approach to education and research production with high accountability demanded of both institutions and individuals. This section has considered three types of reasons why research ethics is important: moral reasons, institutional reasons, and what I term 'practical moral' reasons which both meet moral justifications and 'make sense' in terms of promoting high-quality research and social goals. This section has explained why you personally should be concerned with the ethics of your research. The next section considers which ethical principles you should use to evaluate it.

CASE STUDY: MAKING A FEATURE OUT OF ETHICAL REVIEW

Briony was in the first year of her PhD. Her research aim was to examine the experiences of family members caring for people with learning disabilities (e.g. Down Syndrome). Briony assumed that researching with carers would be less ethically problematic than researching with the 'vulnerable group' itself and her proposal attracted no serious amendments from the departmental ethics committee. However, as she started observing and interviewing families, she became concerned about the way one or two of the carers spoke and behaved towards their family members with learning disabilities. They used names that seemed like friendly 'nicknames' but weren't always very nice. They were also quite physical if, for example, if their relative was having a seizure or needed calming down. Having checked the policy criteria for reporting such instances, she realized that there was a 'grey area' concerning undesirable behaviour, which did not constitute abuse. She discussed the issues with her supervisor and her ethics representative in psychology. These carers had welcomed her into their homes and responded honestly about the real-life difficulties of caring for years on end, including undesirable experiences. If she raised these issues, would they see her as a 'spy' rather than someone who was giving them a voice? On the other hand, perhaps this behaviour could be changed. In the end, Briony was something of an expert on this ethical 'grey area'. She decided to make it a feature of her PhD, devoting one whole chapter on it and used it as the basis for a published paper.

Ethical Dilemma 1: Why do ethical review?

Kendra has just started her master's in public health. She is very involved with a children's home in Kenya, having worked in her gap year out there. She is particularly interested in researching how the staff interact with children who have HIV/AIDS. While she was there last year, she talked with many members of staff, and recorded/took notes of some of the conversations with their permission. Now she has started her master's, her supervisor has told her she cannot use these quotes as she did not have prior ethical approval from her institution. She is frustrated as she will not have the money to return to Kenya before her master's is finished and collect more data. She was also very careful to ask for permission before recording anyone.

1. Why is it important to seek ethical approval before starting data collection?
2. What are the disadvantages of getting ethical approval before starting data collection?
3. Do you think the supervisor's decision is ethical? Why or why not?

---

2 Ethical Principles and Codes

This chapter introduces the basic ethical principles that underlie research ethics, enshrined in paradigmatic codes such as the Nuremberg Code developed after the atrocities of World War II, and the Belmont Report, which set out the legislative requirements for the protection of human subjects in the US (The National Commission for the Protection of Human Subjects of Biomedical and Behavioural Research, 1979). This chapter offers a definition of each principle and considers its main applications in research ethics. These principles and their applications are designed to regulate the researcher–researched relationship to protect the participant, both as an individual and as a member of a group within society. This chapter also considers whether these basic ethical principles are 'universal' (apply across all time-points and cultures) or 'relative' (specific to a given culture) and what the consequences of this might be for ethical practice.

ETHICAL PRINCIPLES

Most professional codes utilize a set of basic ethical principles or values which are theorized to guide decision-making. Although there are slight differences in the core set, they are generally agreed to be: respect for persons (autonomy and protection of the vulnerable), justice (treat people fairly), beneficence (do good), nonmaleficence (do no harm) and fidelity (don't lie, be trustworthy) (e.g. Kitchener & Kitchener, 2009; Shamoo & Resnick, 2009; Sieber, 1992). The first four of these were articulated in the seminal Belmont Report described in the Case Study at the end of this chapter. I also add a sixth principle: academic freedom. These principles are not derived from one ethical theory; rather different principles are derived from different theories (e.g. Kant for autonomy).

Principle 1: Respect for people (autonomy)

There are two main parts to the principle of 'respect for people'. One is that individuals should be treated as autonomous agents. In this context, autonomous means individuals are able to make independent decisions about whether and how they are involved in research. The second is that persons with diminished autonomy, or the incapacity for independent decision-making, are entitled to protection. These persons are called 'vulnerable subjects' within research ethics.

The principle of 'respect for persons' underlies a set of common applied rules or practices within research ethics: informed consent, protection of vulnerable subjects and PAC (privacy, anonymity and confidentiality). 'Informed consent' refers to informing potential participants so that they can make an autonomous decision about whether and how to participate. This has three elements: information (ensuring the person has enough information about the purpose, procedures, risks and benefits of the study to make a decision), comprehension (ensuring the information is understood) and voluntariness (ensuring participation is voluntary and without pressure). Ensuring informed consent is considered a pre-requisite by most researchers, although considerable debates have occurred about how best to achieve it in social research (e.g. Capron, 1982; Miller & Boulton, 2007; Shannon, 2007; Tymchuk, 1997; Wiles, Heath, Crow, & Charles, 2005). Covert research, in which participants do not consent prior to participation and/or are deceived during the study, remains controversial (Herrera, 1999). For more on this, see 'Hot Topic: Informed Consent' (Chapter 7).

The second set of rules derived from 'respect for persons' covers the protection of the vulnerable. There are two aspects to this. The first is to assess whether the person has the capacity to consent (i.e. can understand and process the information and decision to participate). Full capacity is usually assumed. Reasons for impaired capacity could include a brain injury, dementia or having a disability associated with impaired capacity (e.g. learning difficulty). Secondly, research ethics codes have identified 'vulnerable groups' who have additional needs or constraints on their participation in research. Pregnant women, groups with minority or stigmatized social status (e.g. through race, class, poverty, sexuality or age), prisoners or any enclosed group, children, learning disabled, those with psychiatric disorders and others have all been identified as 'vulnerable'. The historical motivation for this classification was the abuse of vulnerable groups in medical research (e.g. see the Case Study in this chapter). However, vulnerable groups should not be excluded from research, as this contravenes the principle of justice. For more on 'Vulnerable Groups and Sensitive Topics', see the relevant Hot Topic (Chapter 10).

The final set of practices/rules that derive from 'respect for persons' is known as PAC (privacy, anonymity and confidentiality). These are discussed in depth in Hot Topics (Chapter 8). For now, it is noted that each of these refers to an aspect of ensuring dignity and respect in the research relationship. Privacy refers to the extent research intrudes into the private world of the participant. Confidentiality refers to the extent to which the collected data, whether interviews, experimental or ethnographic observations, is shared with others or kept private. Preserving anonymity means disguising identifying details of the research participant, with the motivation of ensuring privacy and confidentiality. Again, these have been discussed extensively in relation to their applicability for social research (e.g. Sieber, 1992; Snyder, 2002), and the challenges posed to them by researching on the Internet (Berry, 2004; Burbules, 2009).

Principle 2: Beneficence (benefit)

Beneficence refers to the need to 'do good' in research. Benefits can be direct (i.e. benefit that particular participant) or indirect (i.e. benefit society as a whole by increasing knowledge). Potential benefits could include: increasing knowledge about a phenomenon, benefitting from treatment within a trial, having one's experience represented (having a 'voice' or 'your say') or benefitting from the experience of being researched. Researchers have to balance these benefits against the next principle 'do no harm' (Beauchamp & Childress, 1979). The Nuremberg Code explicitly argues against improving societal knowledge at the expense of the individual participating in a study. The benefits of participation in a particular study are usually explained in the consent procedures, alongside the risks.

Principle 3: Do no harm (nonmaleficence)

'Do no harm' is a key principle derived from medicine. Doing no harm refers to not actively inflicting harm on individuals in the course of research, as well as avoiding the risk of harm. Having said that, 'do no harm' is not an absolute principle. In research, the risks of harm are often balanced against other principles, particularly 'beneficence' (benefit). In other words, there has to be a balance between the potential risks of participating and the benefits, with the balance tipped towards not harming (Beauchamp & Childress, 1979).

One difficulty in implementing 'do no harm' is that conceptually, the notion of 'harm' or 'risk' is vague and ambiguous (Kitchener & Kitchener, 2009). Several definitions are used including the severity, length and typicality of the risk (i.e. is it greater than that which people usually experience in their everyday lives?) These definitions are important, as the level of ethical scrutiny is often tailored to the classified level of risk.

Most researchers and students reading this book will not be doing research which is likely to greatly harm their participants (or at least I hope not!) Indeed, it has been argued that it is wrong to apply medical criterion, in which there may be a small but significant risk of harm or even death, to social research (Jacobsen, Gewurtz, & Haydon, 2007). Personally, I do not find this compelling as a reason for not considering social research in terms of 'harm'. The case of research with the Yamomamo in which a series of anthropologists were accused of harming participants in numerous ways, ranging from sexual abuse to genocide (by introducing the measles virus into a 'virgin' population with no natural immunity) has surely put paid to the notion that social research can never cause harm (Tierney, 2000). Even if all of these allegations were proved false (see Dreger, 2011), they demonstrate that social research, like all spheres of human activity, has the potential to cause harm. However, this is an extreme example. Most social research falls into a 'minimal risk' category of everyday experiences, and as such, may not require full ethical review (see Chapters 3 and 9 for more on the assessment of possible harm).

Principle 4: Justice

This is the third core principle of the Belmont Code. Justice refers to who benefits from the research that is conducted, and who 'bears its burdens', or, in other terms 'takes the risks'? Justice remains an issue within ethical research because of the general power differential between researching institution (which are often wealthy and socially powerful), the researcher (who is often a professional or educated student) and the researched. One of the case studies at the end of this chapter is the Tuskagee study in which poor illiterate African Americans, some with syphilis, were selected for observation over a 40-year period. It has been argued that selecting this group was exploitative, as entering the study was their only way of getting health care (Jones, 1993).

Applying the principle of justice in social research means thinking about who is selected, who is excluded and who benefits in both the long- and short-term. Study procedures should not deliberately or unintentionally exclude certain groups (e.g. women or ethnic groups). Equally, particularly vulnerable groups should not be targeted for research purposes because they are convenient or easy to manipulate (e.g. through poverty). There is concern, for example, that many clinical trials are now conducted in impoverished parts of the world for this reason.

Current action, participatory and transformative approaches go further than simply changing sampling strategies. As discussed in Chapter 1, from these perspectives, the role of social and other scientists is to work for the goals of social justice in an active sense, challenging oppression and discrimination through research, so that the result is a more equal society (e.g. Mertens, 2009; Mertens, Holmes, & Harris, 2009). Reading this literature is a good way of challenging oneself as a researcher to ask: 'what are the goals of my research within a wider societal setting?' and 'who benefits from my research?'

Principle 5: Fidelity (honesty, integrity, trust)

Kitchener and Kitchener (2009) suggest fidelity as a core principle, as it encompasses many other principles important in research relationships, such as honesty, trustworthiness and integrity. When a participant decides to take part in, for example, an experiment or interview study, they have certain expectations of the research relationship. Practices such as confidentiality and anonymity imply trustworthiness and integrity on the part of the researcher. The participant expects the researcher to be honest about the purposes and likely outcomes of their research, one reason why covert research remains ethically problematic (Homan, 1991, 1992).

Similarly, working in collaborative relationships with other researchers is predicated on honesty and trust. Plagiarism, falsifying results or stealing others' ideas devalues the reputation of research at a societal level. Shamoo and Resnick make the important point that these are not just a matter of individual character and conscience. Values such as honesty and integrity are transmitted through ethical leadership at an institutional level; conversely if these are not promoted or acted upon, then dishonest, deceitful, negligent or unlawful practices become the norm (Shamoo & Resnick, 2009, pp. 21–23).

Principle 6: Academic freedom

This principle refers to the freedom of the researcher to be able to design, conduct and disseminate their research freely, without interference. Interference can arise from commercial companies, funding bodies, governments or institutional pressures within universities. At the undergraduate level, academic freedom is not normally a key concern, as choices over which topics to study are often limited to 'low risk' practice research. However, from the masters level upwards, academics may be more constrained. Controversial but valuable research which may attract negative headlines (e.g. into 'difficult' topics such as sex work, terrorism, the police/law enforcement or even research which is critical of current academic practices) may be discouraged on the basis of institutional reputation (e.g. Allen, 2009). Academics may be investigated by the police or other authorities (Adler and Adler, 2002). For example, UK academics researching in the field of 'terrorism studies' (to understand the motivations and practices of terrorism) have been investigated and, in one instance, arrested on the basis of the Terrorism Act (Chomsky et al., 2011). Other constraints on research come from pressures placed by funders or sponsors, such as the pre-screening of publications.

ETHICAL CODES AND GUIDELINES

Codes are sets of ethical rules which are designed to govern professional conduct. Guidelines outline and discuss the problems to be addressed, but not necessarily in a prescriptive way. Ethical codes are divided into several categories. The first category encompasses general codes about research with human subjects, primarily derived from medicine, but covering 'behavioural research' as well. Examples include the Nuremberg Code, the Declaration of Helsinki and the Belmont Report. The second category is disciplinary codes written by the relevant associations (e.g. American Anthropological Association, British Psychological Society). Although these codes are broadly based on the standard principles, they also pay particular attention to the ethical issues within that discipline. For example, in psychological codes, there are rules about debriefing subjects after experiments involving deception (American Psychological Association, 2002; British Psychological Society, 2009). Anthropological codes such as that of the American Anthropological Association emphasize the importance of maintaining integrity in long-term (covenantal) relationships with host families and communities (American Anthropological Association, 1998, updated 2009).

Other codes are cross-disciplinary/cross-national. Examples of this include the Social Research Association code (Social Research Association, 2003), codes from funding bodies such as the Economic and Social Research Council in the UK, and the RESPECT guidelines (Dench, Ifophen, & Huws, 2004) covering socio-economic research in the European Union. Finally, codes have been developed that are specific to particular groups (e.g. the Maori or First Nation people in the US).

These codes not only cover important ethical guidance on how to conduct research with participants, but also on relationships with colleagues, institutions, funders and society at large. Codes also develop over time. For example, concern has grown in the American Anthropological Association about anthropological research conducted with commercial companies or the US military. This has led to amendments in 2009 to the original 1998 Code reiterating the importance of transparency of funding and purpose and on when to withhold research results.

This leads to the question of whether ethical codes are useful. In some disciplines, such as psychology (in which psychologists may be intervening/treating individuals), the Code of Conduct is relatively prescriptive. Serious transgressions may trigger a disciplinary hearing. Other codes are envisaged more as a framework to guide decision-making.

As a student or researcher, it is not necessary to have read all, or even most of these codes to conduct ethical research. However, it makes sense to look at the one or two codes which most closely relate to your research discipline. These represent current thinking about normative ethical practice in that area of which it is important to be aware. They can also be useful to cite if you anticipate needing to justify some aspect of your design to an Institutional Review Board (IRB) or ethics committee. It has been argued that codes are too prescriptive, and their principles too abstract, to encompass the multiple scenarios and interactions which researchers find themselves confronted with in the field (Small, 2001). This is a good point. Principles, as enshrined in codes and guidelines, should represent a starting point for ethical thinking and debate rather than a final word.

For a list of codes, guidelines and resources, see the Appendix.

Quick question

What are the advantages of having an ethics code to follow? What are the disadvantages?

ETHICAL RELATIVISM

Ethical relativism is the idea that ethical or moral truths are not universal ('universalism'), but rather beliefs or norms which reflect the culture in which they originate. Consequently, different cultures have different ethical norms which can be described and compared (descriptive relativism). Some relativists would go further to argue that different ethical perspectives ought to be valued equally as the product of diverse cultures (normative relativism). From this perspective, there is no rationale for preferring Western ethical norms rather than those from non-Western cultures. The implications of this are profound for research ethics. It suggests that our so-called universal ethical principles are in fact culturally bound and may not apply in all cases across all cultures. No one would argue that only Western researchers understand what is moral and acceptable. Should we therefore accept different ethical principles and norms when researching in cultures where these vary from our own? Is it not 'ethnocentric' (seeing one's own culture and rules as the 'gold standard') to do so?

Despite its initial attractiveness as a theory, normative ethical relativism is theoretically problematic. It cannot call any traditions, beliefs or practices 'bad' or 'wrong'. Hinman suggests a middle way between relativism and absolutism in ethics, 'moral pluralism' (Hinman, 2008, pp. 29–30). This meets four intuitions about what it means to be moral: 'understanding' (that we should seek to understand the customs, culture and values of others without necessarily approving), 'tolerance' (that we should prioritize being tolerant of others but not necessarily at the expense of our own values), 'standing up against evil' (where wrongdoing is extreme, it should not be tolerated) and 'fallibility' (we should allow for the possibility that we have got it morally wrong, not other cultures). Although it is relatively easy to criticize this type of moral pluralism at a philosophical level (how can we ever know who is morally wrong between two cultures?), it goes some way to pragmatically redressing the bias towards Western ethno-centrism in ethics.

To take an example, informed consent in Western medical contexts has traditionally meant getting participants to sign a consent form. Critics of this have pointed out that in other contexts and cultures, asking participants to sign written documents can be interpreted as a sign of distrust rather than trust. Furthermore, communities may make decisions at a more collective level rather than as separate individuals. However, differences in how cultures make decisions do not mean that the moral requirement to seek 'informed consent' should be abandoned (Fluehr-Lobban, 2002). Indeed, to not inform participants from different cultures of the purposes of research contradicts the principle of fairness (justice). Rather, procedures must be designed to produce 'informed consent' within that context, using culturally appropriate materials or processes.

However, descriptive relativism takes you so far but no further. As the ethical dilemma at the end of this chapter indicates, there may be times in which you have to decide whose values or which cultural norms to prioritize. Furthermore, principles such as social justice and universal human rights are continually challenged by culturally normative practices (e.g. female genetic mutilation, child brides, over-representation of low-income youth in the military). As a researcher, it is possible to be respectful without agreeing, it is possible to be tolerant without condoning and it is possible to engage in research which fully represents the issue in question for the participants concerned, whilst seeking social change. Sometimes being ethical does mean getting off the fence.

WHAT IS THE RELATIONSHIP BETWEEN THEORIES OF ETHICS, PRINCIPLES AND CODES?

In the last chapter, we examined some of the main philosophical positions connected with ethical theories. How do these relate to standard ethical principles and professional codes, or indeed, to everyday ethical practices? Kitchener and Kitchener suggest a five-level hierarchical model of ethical decision-making to explain this relationship (Kitchener & Kitchener, 2009). At the bottom of the model (Level 1) are 'particular cases' which are the everyday ethical scenarios researchers find themselves in, which require information about the situation and what they term 'ordinary moral sense' (a sense of morality developed over time as part of our character). Above these are 'ethical rules' (Level 2), which are the norms or conventions of practice within professional codes (e.g. gaining informed consent). At Level 3 are 'ethical principles', which are more general than the rules, but provide justification for them. Beyond this (Level 4) are 'ethical theories', such as the deontological, natural rights and utilitarianism, which provide a basis for reasoning when moral dilemmas arise. The final level (Level 5) is 'meta-ethics', which reflects on the meaning of ethics itself. They suggest that where ordinary moral decision-making fails, one should look up the tiers of the model to more critically evaluate the dilemma at hand. If there is no direction in professional codes, then appealing to meta-theories is one way of resolving this (e.g. by considering the motivations or outcomes of a certain research practice).

However, it is not clear everyone has the same 'ordinary moral sense'. Occasionally, people do things that appear to completely defy it (e.g. take advantage of participants' circumstances, steal data from colleagues). One reason that ethical codes and principles are useful is to set out a set of common expectations. We can then all debate whether they apply in a particular situation from that basis.

SUMMARY

Principles and codes are essentially normative (agreed within a given group) and abstract (present a general rule which may or not apply in a given scenario). The real-life practice of research may lead to contradictory principles coming into play; ethical codes may also say little about common-place occurrences, such as a participant crying in an interview. Codes and principles are also culturally bound and require cultural sensitivity in their interpretation. Nevertheless, a sound knowledge of the main principles and relevant codes makes a starting point for ethical thinking and discussion. The next chapter looks at how institutions interpret and review research based on these principles.

CASE STUDY: ETHICAL 'HORROR STORIES' AND THE DEVELOPMENT OF CODES

In the twentieth century, the need for regulation of medical ethics was brought into sharp focus by the unethical experimentation on human subjects by the Nazis during World War II. Concentration camp prisoners, including Jews, homosexuals, mentally disabled, physically disabled and aged individuals, took part in medical experimentation without their consent 'in the course of which experiments the defendants committed murders, brutalities, cruelties, tortures, atrocities, and other inhuman acts' (Indictment, 1949–53). For example, hypothermia experiments involved immersing the subjects in freezing water until they died. The Nuremberg Doctors Trial of 1946 resulted in seven of the 23 men being executed for crimes against humanity. Similar torture and experimentation on humans took place in the Japanese military (Unit 731). The debate over whether there could ever be the ethical use of the results of such experimentation has never been resolved (e.g. Rosner et al., 1991; Ziporyn, 1990). One result was the production of the Nuremberg Code (1948), which established internationally recognized standards for the protection of human subjects in research (Annas & Grodin, 1992). Although other codes, such as the Declaration of Helsinki (1964 and 2000) and the Belmont Report (1979), have built on it, the principles of informed consent and the protection of the vulnerable enshrined in the Nuremberg Code remain as the basic building blocks of research ethics.

The Tusgekee syphilis study also represents an ethical 'horror story'. The US Public Health service recruited hundreds of low-income illiterate African American males from the South, most of whom had syphilis, into the study in 1932, with promises of medical care. Their aim was to see how the disease progressed in this particular group and they were monitored for the next 40 years. Researchers did not inform their participants that they had syphilis, rather gave them misinformation about having conditions related to a catch-all term, 'bad blood' (Jones, 1993). Furthermore, when an effective treatment (penicillin) became available in the 1940s for syphilis, the researchers did not offer it to the men. Although questions were raised about the ethics of the study for many years, the study only finally ended in 1972 after media exposure. President Clinton apologized to the remaining participants and their families in 1997. This 40-year study remains in the literature as a classic example of the abuse of the vulnerable subject, as well as of racism in medical research. Indeed, it has been argued that the distrust that was sown in the

African American community about the medical profession has made it harder to tackle subsequent epidemics such as HIV (Jones, 1993). As with the Nuremberg trials, this study pushed forward the legal protection of participants, with the establishment of the National Commission for the Protection of Human Subjects of Biomedical and Behavioural Research who produced the Belmont Report (1979), which underlies our ethical codes and regulations today. The Tuskagee study is usually considered a classic ethical 'horror story', although recent re-examination of it suggest that it may be more morally complex than it was first thought to be (Hammersley, 2006, p. 7; Shweder, 2004).

Ethical Dilemma 2: Cultural relativism

Ashia is doing a master's in women's studies at a European university, but her data collection will take place in her home country in the Middle East. Her fieldwork will be participant observation of women's daily lives as they go about cooking, childcare and other activities, and she will personally be participating alongside the women for three months. In this culture at this timepoint, men have significant power over women to make decisions in their lives. Traditionally, husbands would be asked for permission for their wives to participate in medical treatment or taking part in research. The ethical principle of autonomy and respect for persons is usually interpreted in terms of asking individuals for their informed consent. Ashia is intending to seek informed consent from the women themselves, but she is unsure if she should also ask their husbands' permission first.

1. Which ethical principles are involved in making this decision?
2. Who do you think Ashia should seek consent from and why?
3. Does it make a difference that Ashia comes from that particular culture herself? Why?
4. What would a 'social justice' perspective that privileges the voice of the less powerful add to this ethical dilemma?

---

3 Ethical Procedures, Institutions and Norms

This chapter focuses on 'procedural ethics' (Guillemin & Gillam, 2004). Although ethics procedures differ between institutions and countries, the basic process is similar. Written applications or 'protocols' describing research projects are submitted for ethical review to groups of designated individuals (called 'ethics committees' or 'Institutional Review Boards' [IRBs]), and the research projects have to be approved by the designated group before research can start. This chapter outlines the structure of ethics procedures in a number of countries (UK, US, Canada, Australia and others) where ethics review is well-established. Your own institution's specific requirements will fit within these wider structures (see Chapter 5 for more on how to write a high-quality proposal and gain ethical approval). This chapter also examines the numerous criticisms which have been made of current ethics review systems.

WHAT ARE IRBS OR ETHICS COMMITTEES?

Different terms are used in different countries for the groups that make decisions about ethical review. In the US, they are known as Institutional Review Boards (or IRBs), in the UK as research ethics committees (RECs) and in Canada research ethics boards (REBs). Despite the differences in terminology, they are constructed and behave in similar ways.

> **Quick question**
>
> *Who should sit on IRBs or ethics committees? What qualifies someone to judge whether other people's research is ethical?*

An ethics board or committee is a group formed to review the ethical aspects of research and clinical interventions/trials with humans and/or animals. Social research with subjects is typically reviewed by boards/committees with a remit to protect their human rights, welfare and dignity. As a collective body, boards/committees are required to be independent from the research they review. It would be unethical, for example, if they only supported research which they personally liked or funded by their own employers. Their independence is determined by several criteria: having many members (so decisions are made collectively, not by one individual), abiding by strict rules around conflicts of interests (so removing the possibility of biased judgement) and being accountable (so allowing others to see the decisions made and to challenge them formally if appropriate). They should also be made up of men and women (e.g. ESRC, 2010, p. 12) and of people from different racial, cultural and community groups (45 CRF 46.107, 1981). However, not all IRBs/RECs meet these criteria.

All IRBs/committees have a Chair who leads the group and can make decisions on their own if there are not enough other members available or a project needs urgent or 'expedited' review (Chair's Action). The Chair also signs off amendments (changes to the original project submission) to say they are accepted and usually signs the certificate of approval.

The rest of the committee are made up of individual members drawn from the institution or research centre. If it is an academic committee, members may come either all from one discipline in large departments or from multiple disciplines; inter-disciplinary groups are preferred as they bring a variety of perspectives and norms (ESRC, 2010, p. 12). Within medical institutions members will primarily be clinicians and managers. There is often one or more 'lay members' who are ordinary people who have some interest in ethics (e.g. member of the clergy, patient representative) and can provide an alternative view.

There is also an IRB administrator or committee secretary. This is a very important role, as they collate and administer the applications, send them out for review and are the main point of contact between researchers and the IRB/committee.

Institutions frequently have hierarchies of ethics boards/committees. For example, a university may have a University Ethics Committee, which oversees ethical issues across the institution, for example, determining the overall ethics policy, deciding which funding is ethical to accept or whether animal experimentation should be allowed. There may then be a set of sub-committees within the different colleges/departments which deal with applications from their own staff and students. These hierarchies mean that any unresolved or disputed applications can be sent upwards for advice or for appeals.

IRBs/RECs may come across types of research or ethical dilemmas with which they are unfamiliar. If they lack expertise, they should seek external advice, such as from experts in a particular methodology, legal services, information technology, human resources or other IRBs/ethics committees. Many IRBs/REC also require projects to be of a good academic standard (e.g. demonstrated by submitting peer reviews) although for student and postgraduate applications, this may not be required.

HOW ARE PROJECTS APPROVED?

Ethics review takes place prior to starting the research project, and is known as 'anticipatory review'. A 'protocol' or 'project proposal' is written which specifies what will happen in the research, an 'official account' of the planned research. This includes the research goals, which methods will be used, who are the participants, how the sample will be recruited and what will happen in the research (procedure). There are then sections, typically but not exclusively, on informed consent, anonymity and confidentiality, assessment of possible harms/benefits, data protection, conflict of interests and possibly insurance.

Retrospective applications (i.e. where data collection has already begun) are not usually allowed. It is very important that ethics review is completed before you intend to start your research. As outlined in Chapter 1, failure to have your research ethically reviewed is now viewed very negatively. You may jeopardize your course completion, your PhD award or journal acceptance if you do not gain ethical approval and/or cannot prove this in the form of a certificate.

IRBs/committees usually meet several times a year to consider applications. Having read them in advance, they then discuss them either face-to-face, or increasingly, electronically. There are several potential outcomes: (a) approved without changes, (b) amendments requested, which are changes the researchers are expected to make to gain approval or (c) rejected. Outright rejection, with no possibility of resubmission, is a rare outcome only reserved for projects which are incomplete, illegal or cannot meet minimum ethical standards.

IRBs and ethics committees are increasingly being called to account, as their decision-making processes are 'behind closed doors' (Stark, 2011). Some IRBs/ethics committees publish 'audits' listing how many applications they have had and how many were passed with or without amendments, but few other details of decisions. IRBs/ethics committees should have a transparent appeals process through which applicants can request further clarification or disagree with their decision-making. However, in practice, the committee's decision is often tacitly understood by all involved as final. If there is not a visible appeals process for your IRB/ethics committee, any serious disagreements should be put in writing to the Chair.

For more on how to write high-quality ethics proposals and navigate the review process, see Chapter 5.

'MINIMAL RISK' REVIEW

Many ethics review processes operate within a two-tier system known as 'minimal risk' or 'light touch' review. These can also be known as 'low-risk/high-risk' pathways or a 'two-track' system. Essentially, these systems aim to tailor the level of review to the level of risk. Lower risk proposals which are intrinsically less problematic receive a 'light touch' review, with full attention paid to higher risk proposals which are reviewed by the full committee.

'Minimal risk' for the purposes of choosing a track usually refers to (a) the risk of experiencing harm outside of the usual experiences of participants and (b) the lack of risk of substantive harm (e.g. that is physically or psychologically long-lasting beyond the research situation). A fuller discussion of the definitions is provided in Hot Topics Chapter 9. The decision over which projects or proposals fall into the 'minimal risk' category is not standardized. Most IRBs/ethics committees produce a checklist or set of criteria, which sets out their interpretation of 'minimal risk'. In general, all research with vulnerable groups and with children under 18 (in the US) does not fall under the 'minimal risk' definition and so goes to full review.

In the UK, the Economic and Social Research Council lists sixteen criteria which may indicate full review, including research with vulnerable groups (e.g. children, cognitive impairments, or in an unequal power relationship with the researcher such as your students), the use of gatekeepers, covert research, sensitive topics (e.g. sexual activity, drug use), administering substances, taking tissue sample, causing more than mild pain or psychological stress beyond that encountered in normal life, prolonged testing, the use of secure or controlled data, researcher safety, members of the public (e.g. participant observation), research outside the UK, internet research, sharing confidential data beyond the initial consent period (e.g. archiving) or financial inducements beyond reasonable compensation for time and travel (ESRC ref, pp. 33–34).

If you work, as I do, in a college with several hundred international students all doing dissertations in their home non-UK countries, educational research with children or with members of the public, almost every single social research project would be incorporated into this very wide definition of 'high risk'. In practice, institutions often create robust standardized ethical procedures to avoid a committee having to discuss every single instance of very similar research. For example, in education, practice-based research in teaching courses may be reviewed using a short form, an institutional signatory and a CRB (Criminal Records Bureau) check, to distinguish it from other instances of research with children that require greater scrutiny, such as research in care institutions or with homeless teens.

Other institutions may use an exemption criterion based on methodology, for example, exempting research using observation, interviews, surveys and experiments except where there is a greater than minimal risk.

If you are unsure which track (low/high, minimal/full review) your project should follow, read the relevant IRB/ethics committee guidelines which often specify this explicitly. If you are still unsure, contact the relevant administrator or secretary. Finally, remember that 'minimal risk' or 'light touch' review does not mean no review. You usually have to fill out a 'minimal risk' or 'initial checklist' form and provide other documents so that the IRB or committee can certify that your application is going through the right track. They also reserve the right to ask you to switch to full review.

How to assess and discuss risks and benefits within ethics protocols/applications is covered in Hot Topic Chapter 9.

EXPEDITED REVIEW

Expedited review should not be confused with a 'light touch' or 'minimal risk' process. Expedited review is a full review of the protocol/application but done in a short time frame (e.g. if funders require a certificate before releasing funds). It is often done by the Chair and another member of the board/committee.

DOES ALL SOCIAL RESEARCH HAVE TO BE REVIEWED?

Primary research is where you, the researcher, collect the data from human participants. Most primary research with humans is reviewed. Secondary data analysis (e.g. of a dataset with no identification of names/addresses or archive material) may be exempt. Online research is more contentious (see Hot Topics) and advice should be sought from your institution on whether to submit an application; most still consider this primary research. Public observation, where the public are not identified, may also be either exempt (as in Canada) or fall into a minimal risk category exempt from full review. Similarly, classroom research only for learning (pedagogical) purposes is often exempt (e.g. in the US). Oral history has also exempted itself from IRB review in the US. Even if your research project is technically exempt from review, check whether you still need to submit a protocol for the records.

Pilot studies are conducted to test aspects of your research procedures or to establish contacts in the field. In most cases, having non-recorded conversations with key individuals in your research field, or trying out a questionnaire on a few friends to see if the questions make sense does not require review. Pilot work which is similar to a full-scale study (e.g. recorded interviews to be transcribed) but just small scale, or which has a higher risk aspect, may well need review. If you are unsure, check with the relevant ethics administrator.

Many funding bodies in both the UK and US will not release funds until full approval is given. This can be problematic if approval takes months and the money is required for salaries. One solution is to warn the IRB/ethics committee of a pending application, then submit for provisional approval with a full application made immediately as the study starts.

REVIEW OF ETHICAL REGULATIONS IN SELECTED COUNTRIES

The United Kingdom

In the UK, a distinction is drawn between NHS-based and other types of research. It is an evolving system, with NHS committees set up to cover clinical and medical research and only covering social research later on, and universities developing their own systems in the past few years (Stark & Hedgecoe, 2010).

Certain types of social research with particular groups go through the National Research Ethics Service (NRES) for approval by RECs. This includes all research with NHS patients or service users recruited through NHS pathways (e.g. doctors surgeries or from hospital lists), research in social care funded by the Department of Health, research legally requiring REC approval (e.g. for impaired capacity to consent groups) and where standard care is withdrawn. The Central Office for Research Ethics Committees (COREC) coordinates RECs, which include Local Research Ethics Committees (LRECs) serving a particular region, MRECs (which cover multi-site projects) and a new Social Care Committee. Another recent change is the exemption of research with NHS staff from

NHS review; this can now go through regular institutional channels. All research within the health and social care systems and within the public health remit is also covered by the Research Governance Framework. This lays out the ethical standards and governance expected from health and social care organizations (whether public or private) engaged in research, including the structure and processes of ethics committees (http://www.dh.gov.uk/en/PublicationsandstatisticsPublicationsPublicationsPolicyAndGuidance/DH_4108962, accessed 17 May 2012).

Making an application through the NRES system typically takes longer and is more bureaucratic than university systems. This can be a deterrent for students and others on a limited time scale. There have been promises of change towards a brief review system for minimal risk (or 'no material ethical issues') projects (Stark & Hedgecoe, 2010). These are not currently in place. The case study at the end of this chapter looks at a typical experience for a PhD student using the NHS system. Getting through both the NHS ethical and governance procedures took the first year of the PhD. Having said that, there is extensive online guidance and NHS committee administrators/Chairs are usually happy to give advice before submission. Anyone who thinks they need NHS ethics review should contact their local NHS Ethics Service to get advice, forms and a timetable as slots have to be booked in advance.

All other social research is reviewed by university or college committees. Minimum standards of ethical review are required by funding bodies such as the Economic and Social Research Council (ESRC) for institutions which use its funding for centres, projects and studentships. They also outline expectations such as having the ethics policy of the institution on the website, having an appeals procedure and some type of auditing of committee decisions.

The approval of only one body is required for any given piece of research. If you are working on a project with more than one institution or funder involved, then you need to agree to use one institution as the site of review. Similarly, if a project is going through the NHS or Social Care Research Ethics Services, then you do not need to submit a fresh application to your university, though some may like a copy of the paperwork as notification for their files.

University ethical review in the UK is an evolving process in which there is little standardization. A masters project in one institution could be reviewed fully by an entire committee using a long form, be signed off as a short 'minimal risk' project using one page of documentation in another, or viewed as practice research and not reviewed at all. For this reason, both students and staff should clarify very carefully the ethical procedures in their particular institution.

US

In 1974, the federal government made provision for the establishment of IRBs at all universities that accept funding from the Department of Health and Human Services (DHHS). Having an IRB in research institutions, and submitting research for review, is thus enshrined in law. All human research needs to be submitted for review, although classroom research for teaching purposes and other types of research can be exempt (see Title 45 CRF Part 46.101). However, as discussed above, most IRBs have 'minimal risk' systems in which only protocols containing substantive risk have to go for full review.

Although IRBs follow federal regulations governing the protection of human subjects (Title 45 Code of Federal Regulations Part 46), they also devise their own policies and forms to use. These are usually available online or from the IRB administrator. It is thus a decentralized system in which IRBs have considerable autonomy to interpret regulations and devise new requirements (Sieber, 2000). Most IRBs use 'local precedents' so new protocols are treated in similar ways to previous ones (Stark, 2011). As in the UK, norms of ethical review for certain types of research (e.g. for children or qualitative research) can differ between different IRBs, even if federal rules are followed. Getting information on the previous handling of similar research protocols in that IRB and citing relevant literature can both help establish that what you are proposing fits within existing ethical norms. Another issue within the US system is determining which IRB to ask for approval. Multiple IRBs may need to be involved in certain projects which can alter time-scales for research.

Canada

Canada has a relatively similar system of ethics boards and review to the US using research ethics boards ('REBs'). Boards follow the principles set out in the Tri-Council Policy Statement on Ethical Conduct for Research Involving Humans, which was launched in 1998 and has recently been updated in 2010 (TCPS 2) (CIHR at al., 2010). This is a policy agreed by the main research bodies of the Canadian Institute for Health Research (CIHR, formerly MRC), the Natural Sciences and Engineering Research Council of Canada (NSERC) and the Social Science and Humanities Research Council (SSHRC). Although the comprehensiveness of producing a national ethics policy to cover all disciplines has been lauded, as elsewhere some social scientists have expressed concerns about using a natural science model to assess ethics in social research (Kellner, 2002).

Australia

Australia also has a developed system of ethical review of all research with human subjects through Human Research Ethics Committees (HRECS). These are overseen by the Australian Health Ethics Committee (AHEC) and are established within institutions such as hospitals as well as universities. Not all research organizations have HRECs; some use those of other institutions. The structure, governance and policies of human ethics review in Australia are laid out in the National Statement on Ethics Conduct in Human Research (NHMRC, 2007). One problem is the ongoing need for multiple reviews in collaborative projects, which takes much time and delays starting research. There have been recent moves to simplify this under a single national review process. Reviews undertaken with one committee (e.g. a hospital ethics committee for a project involving patients) may also need to be registered elsewhere (e.g. university ethics committee).

Other countries which have comprehensive ethics review systems include New Zealand and Nordic countries such as Denmark and Sweden.

DEVELOPING COUNTRIES AND CROSS-CULTURAL ETHICS REVIEW

Many countries do not have any formal ethics review procedures for social scientists. In these instances, the onus is on you, to use your ethical sense and use appropriate ethical procedures.

However, equally, you should not assume developing countries or communities have no ethical structures or processes. Most countries have regulations and guidelines in relation to the conduct of clinical trials. Communities may also have decision-making bodies (e.g. tribal authorities or district government) which decide whether to give permission for researchers to conduct research in a given location. For social researchers not engaged in clinical or medical research, it is not always clear to whom to apply for permission. There are currently no international standards of ethics for global research (Fluehr-Lobban, 2002). However, the onus is on the researcher to visit the location in advance, speak with other researchers working in that location and negotiate with key gatekeepers (people who allow access to a particular research field or site). Ethical review may look different if the decision to host a researcher is discussed in a series of meetings with village elders rather than submitted in a Word file to a committee. However, it is essentially the same process of prior ethical review; considering how to ensure the rights of the participants, and to consider the wider implications of research for the community as a whole. Examples of community consent with indigenous groups are available on the World Health Organization website (see Appendix).

It can be slightly problematic if you are based in one country, but the site of research is in another. Many countries require an ethics certificate from the originating institution for the project. Occasionally, ethics approval in the second country may be required (e.g. if researching within their health care system). Issues can arise where ethical requirements or regulations conflict. To take an example, an IRB/ethics committee in the originating country may not appreciate the cultural issues around asking participants to sign a document in another culture. In some cultures, refusing to sign researchers' forms is a way of asserting authority for that particular group (Shannon, 2007). However, as Fluehr-Lobban has forcefully argued, negotiating ethics is as important in non-Western countries as Western countries (Fluehr-Lobban, 2002). It should not be assumed that it represents some form of ethnocentric imperialism to ask people's permission to take part in research, even if the language or form of consent is adapted to suit the culture. How to create robust consent procedures in different cultures is discussed further in Hot Topics (Chapter 7).

CRITIQUES OF IRBS AND ETHICS COMMITTEES

An extensive critique of the current formal systems of ethics review has grown up in the literature. As Halse and Honey state, ethical review has become an 'institutional discourse' in which what is considered 'ethical' is constructed in a very specific way within universities, hospitals and public organizations (Halse & Honey, 2007, p. 337). For many, the surveillance and regulation of social research through current research ethics systems is overly restrictive (Hammersley, 2006; Murphy & Dingwall, 2007; Haggerty, 2004; Beh, 2002). Some key points of the critique are as follows:

- *The bureaucratic nature of system.* Research ethics review can be both time-consuming and overly bureaucratic. It can significantly delay research projects particularly if multiple or highly complex administrative procedures have to be followed, involving lengthy submission forms and procedures. This may delay important or socially beneficial research occurring, contrary to ethical principles (Hall, 1991). This criticism has been made extensively by medical and clinical researchers, not just social scientists (e.g. Ahmed & Nicholson, 1996).
- *Inappropriateness of using systems from clinical medicine to review social research.* As the case study in Chapter 2 showed, ethical regulations were originally designed to protect human subjects within medical and clinical research. It has been argued that appropriating these practices for the review of social research is inappropriate in a variety of ways, particularly where the methods and epistemological beliefs underlying the research are dissimilar, such as in qualitative or participatory research (Lincoln & Tierney, 2004). For example, the practice of 'anticipatory review' makes sense within medical or

clinical research, as the research design requires hypotheses to be specified in advance, and the procedure to be standardized in protocols for use across multiple clinical sites. However, in qualitative and ethnographic studies, the researcher may deliberately keep many of these aspects open as the research begins, for example, adapting interview questions in a reflexive manner, or interviewing different individuals as the focus of research is refined (Dingwall, 2006; Murphy & Dingwall, 2007). Participatory research, in which the research is iterative and developed as part of a collaborative process with participants, may run into difficulties with IRBs for precisely this reason (Boser, 2007). Another example of the potential mismatch between medical and social research practices is the use of one-off consent procedures. Written forms may 'make sense' within a hospital administration system (although many medical ethicists have critiqued the length of them), but may be either culturally inappropriate, or not a suitable method for ensuring informed consent in longer-term participant–researcher relationships (Boulton & Parker, 2007). The concept of 'harm' derived from medicine has also been argued to be inappropriately applied to social science ethical review, as discussed in Chapter 2.

- *The restrictiveness of the 'audit' culture.* Ethics review processes are part of a wider 'audit' culture that has developed within academic life and elsewhere, in which academic freedom is restricted, and the scope for the regulation of research is ever widened. Haggerty calls this 'ethics creep', the process by which activities which previously were not considered research, or potentially harmful, have come under the expansion of ethics regulation (Haggerty, 2004; see also Lincoln & Tierney, 2004).

- *Questioning of the motivation for ethical review.* IRBs and ethics committees have been argued to be increasingly concerned with institutional reputation rather than human participant protection. Research which may attract controversy, or is legally complex (e.g. into sex work (Roberts, Bergstrom, & La Rooy, 2007) or terrorism studies) may be deterred by the difficulties of facing ethical review or receive amendments/rejection, which make the research untenable.

- *Inability to challenge the system.* The institutional authority of IRBs and ethics committees is very high, bolstered by funders, organizations and disciplinary bodies who require acceptance of their decision-making as a condition of being a researcher or releasing funds. It is very difficult for researchers to challenge the decision-making of boards and committees within this context (Dixon-Woods, Angell, Ashcroft, & Bryman, 2007).

● *Lack of consistency.* IRBs and ethics committees can make inconsistent and unsystematic decisions, as well as develop different norms within each board/committee (Stark, 2011). The same piece of research can be treated very differently depending where it goes for ethical review (Angell et al., 2006; Redshaw et al., 1996, although see Haggerty, 2004 for the argument that consistency for consistency's sake in ethics protocols is not necessarily desirable).

Suggestions on how to improve IRB and committee review for social research have ranged from calls to resist the audit culture and pressures to conform to a medical model of institutional review (e.g. Hammersley, 2006), for social researchers to join IRBs (Eissenberg et al., 2004), to better educate IRBs and committees about social science (Oakes, 2002) and to set up social science IRBs/committees within universities to give social scientists a 'voice' in ethical review. I favour the latter option, as I think reviewing by peers within social science, particularly by a multi-disciplinary group, offers the necessary expertise and authority.

It is important for students and researchers who will have to submit their work for ethical review to boards and committees to be aware of these critiques. They go to explain why some academics are either openly hostile or contemptuous of ethical review procedures. Furthermore, they highlight that ethics review has not developed in a vacuum, but as part of a historical and political process. It is still changing. For this reason, teachers and professors who themselves did little training in ethics may not feel confident giving extensive advice. Expected knowledge and cultures around ethics have changed considerably in a short time period.

These critiques also point to some of the potential difficulties that students or researchers may face when engaged with ethical review. Many of these criticisms are well-evidenced and well-founded. I agree the prospect of ethical review can deter certain types of research and thus restrict academic freedom. For example, few students at undergraduate or master's level in the UK, who might want to undertake something as simple as interviewing patients at a local GP's surgery, would have the time to gain NHS approval given their course timelines. Furthermore, a focus on formal ethical review undoubtedly leads both institutions and staff/students to believe that they have 'done' ethics once they have approval, whereas in my experience, ethical problems often emerge after approval in an unpredictable way, and often without the necessary institutional support to discuss or resolve them.

Having said that, I do not think that students or researchers should necessarily anticipate they will personally face difficulties when seeking ethical review. Hedgecoe undertook an analysis of three clinical REC's decision-making in the UK where medical models might be expected to be most entrenched (Hedgecoe, 2008a). It revealed no ideological bias against qualitative research, which was dealt with sensitively and flexibly. For every one anecdote given in the ethics literature of a researcher whose research was rejected by an IRB, hundreds of applications go through boards and committees each year with little delay. Procedures are also developing all the time. For example, many committees/IRBs are now realizing that it is not possible to pre-specify interview questions and that a degree of flexibility is appropriate. Others are moving to quicker online systems. I agree with Hedgecoe (2008a) that many institutions seem to be interested in reducing both the bureaucracy and requirements for review, contrary to Haggerty's claim of expansionism. However, overall these critiques have been valuable for pointing out the limits of current practices and suggesting how ethics review might change for the better.

SUMMARY

This chapter has taken an in-depth look at the procedural systems of ethical review which have developed in the past 30 years and which are still developing. In the US, Canada, UK and elsewhere, formal ethical review of social research by boards and committees is relatively common, although not all research is necessarily subject to full review. Guidelines for developing country ethical procedures are also available. The use of IRBs and ethics committees to review social science has been criticized, namely for introducing further bureaucracy, using inappropriate rules and procedures derived from medical science, and stifling academic freedom. Some of these criticisms are truer for some IRBs/committees than for others. Despite this, there is a strong rationale for ethical review as part of a wider system of ethical practice within institutions. Part II of this book now moves on to offer practical advice on gaining ethical approval and the practice of everyday research ethics.

CASE STUDY: TAKING QUALITATIVE RESEARCH THROUGH THE HEALTH-CARE ETHICS SYSTEM

Ryan was a PhD student I was co-supervising, who had a particular interest in genetic conditions in families. When the opportunity came up to interview family groups with a specific genetic disorder, located through a hospital consultant who had worked with these families for decades, he was very enthusiastic. In the UK, any research with patients has to go to a Local Research Ethics Committee (LREC) and not through the quicker university ethics committee route. Although he didn't want all of his participants to come via the consultant (as less severe cases tended to either be undiagnosed or monitored within general practice), he decided to make an NHS application. I knew from previous experience that the form was long; his final submission was over 50 pages long, with another 50 pages of interview schedules and forms attached (it now uses an online system). It was a relatively straightforward interview study, but with a few ethical issues presented by the family dimension, for example, confidentiality was harder to guarantee for a family with a distinctive illness profile. After submission, I attended the committee's face-to-face meeting with the student, which was more intimidating than we had expected, with 12 members quizzing him on various aspects of the project's design and ethics. In line with Hedgecoe (2008a), we found the members sympathetic to qualitative research methods and only minor amendments were requested. This, however, was not the end of the ethics review story. A further few months of NHS governance processes followed (even though he was insured by the university and was interviewing off-site in people's homes), including peer review, more documents and an invite to complete a two-day Health and Safety course including lifting. It took over a year before any research could begin. My conclusion is that although the health care ethics system appears not to be ideologically opposed to qualitative research, it is overly bureaucratic, out of all proportion to the risk of interviewing some consenting adults about their illness experiences.

Ethical Dilemma 3: Student ethical review

Kevin is doing a third-year project on what male university students think about their health. He has done 30 questionnaires and did his first interview of five today. At Kevin's university, third-years do not have to submit a full application to the psychology ethics committee unless projects come into certain 'higher risk' categories, such as sensitive topics or vulnerable groups. Kevin ticked the box stating that his interviews covered neither, as did his supervisor, but now he is not so sure. Much of the interview with the first male interviewee covered his sex life, use (or not) of contraception and even his drug use. Kevin feels out of his depth and is worried that he made the wrong choice of review pathway (low risk when it was higher risk). However, if he puts in an application now, he won't finish his data collection on time to submit his project.

1. Is it unethical for Kevin to go ahead with his interviews? What should he do next?
2. What are the benefits and problems of reviewing student research through formal ethical review channels?
3. Do you agree that reviewing ethical protocols (by IRB's/committees or departments) ensures higher standards of ethical behaviour?

Part II
Ethics in Practice

4 Research Design and Ethics

This chapter, the first of three that focus on the practical issues of human participant research, focuses on research design. I start by outlining the 'lifecycle' approach to research ethics. From this perspective, research ethics is important throughout the 'lifecycle' of a project, from consideration of the initial topic, the design and funding of the study, the choice of participants, through to how results are presented and disseminated. This chapter also considers ethical dilemmas thrown up within research design, from 'should some topics be taboo to research?' or 'do I have an obligation to disseminate my results?' to 'should I report research fraud?' The aim is not to list a set of ethical 'practices' within design (which is not possible) but rather to show that ethical dilemmas and considerations emerge throughout research design, sometimes in unexpected ways. The example of Eva's research with older adults with memory difficulties is used to illustrate these ethical issues.

Example: Eva's project

Eva is a postgraduate student who currently works in one of a group of care/nursing homes for older adults on the weekend. Some of these adults are experiencing cognitive decline, particularly in relation to memory. Although she enjoys working there, she can see ways in which the care of residents could be improved, and feels strongly that their voice needs to be heard. With the owner's permission, she has decided to conduct a small-scale qualitative research project with a similar group of residents from a nearby home to find out how they experience their current care. Her aim is to increase understanding of the needs and perspectives of care home residents with the goal of encouraging improvement at a macro (policy/academic) and micro (recommendations for this specific organization) level.

THE 'LIFECYCLE' APPROACH TO RESEARCH ETHICS

Research ethics as a topic is often detached from other aspects of research design. It is often presented separately in books on research methods from the choice of the method or plan of dissemination (how and where to distribute the findings). However, increasingly, research ethics, or rather, ethics in practice, is understood as something which is embedded in the research process itself. From this perspective, ethics and research are indivisible, and the choices you make about research design have inherently ethical aspects (e.g. Clegg & Slife, 2009).

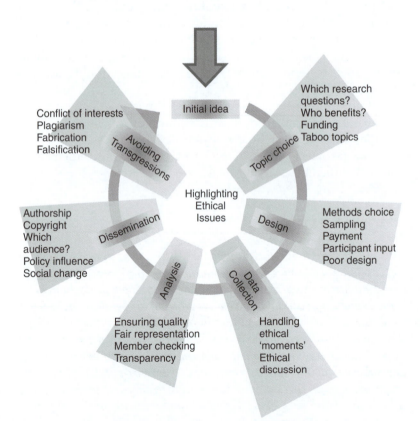

Figure 4.1 Ethics in the research life cycle.

I take what I call a 'lifecycle' approach to research ethics, shown in Figure 4.1. The 'lifecycle' approach refers to planning in business for the entire 'lifecycle' of a product, from the initial idea and design stage through to market saturation and (possibly) decline. Research ethics is not something complete by the writing of an ethics proposal, and over once you receive approval. It is about what you choose to research (topic) and how you choose to conduct it (method). It covers the running of the project (ongoing ethical dilemmas) and what you do with the results afterwards (dissemination). It is also about avoiding ethical transgressions, such as making up data or not declaring a conflict of interests. Other approaches, such as the transformative approach, also conceptualize ethics in terms of the entire project, but in terms of the overall goal, to promote 'social justice' (e.g. Mertens et al., 2009, pp. 96–97). Hammersley (1999) has pointed to the danger of prioritizing ethics above other values such as research quality. My opinion is that producing knowledge involves ethical aspects that are not contained within written forms and deserve reflection; the lifecycle approach is a systematic way to approach ethics. It is important to note that the ethical issues presented in this chapter, illustrated in Figure 4.1, are not exhaustive. Others may come up within the lifecycle of a project. The point is to understand research ethics as the practice of research, examined through an ethical lens, across time.

CHOICE OF TOPIC

Choosing a research question or topic is often discussed in methods texts (White, 2009), but less often from an ethical perspective. This is perhaps surprising given that within wider bioethical discussions, much attention is paid to what constitutes 'legitimate' or 'ethical' research (e.g. should research into embryonic stem cells or animal experimentation be allowed?). There are two issues that are raised choosing a research topic in relation to ethics. One is whether there are some topics which you consider unethical. The other is whether there are any ethical principles you want to promote though the research. Both refer to the ethical values which underlie research questions.

The ethics (or not) of studying certain topics remain contentious. Examples of this include research into variables such as race and intelligence or attractiveness. In 2011, an evolutionary psychologist, Satoshi Kanazawa, at the London School of Economics hit the headlines by doing research into which races were considered more attractive and linking this back to evolutionary features. It was widely considered racist (as well as not very good science; Kaufman & Wicherts, 2011). However, does this mean, therefore, that we should never research race in this way? Psychological work on IQ and race has also proved to be explosive (e.g. the controversial book by Hernstein & Murray (1994). Some people have argued that given the history of eugenics, no research into race and intelligence should be conducted as it will always be used for nefarious purposes (Rose, 2009). Others have argued that it is part of academic freedom to be able to engage with such research and that one cannot always (or should not) predict in advance the outcomes and their consequences (Ceci & Williams, 2009). This links to a more general point that you may not always have control over what happens to one's research, once it has been published, particularly in the digital age (Burbules, 2009).

Another way of looking at the same question is to ask: 'which values and whose interests are promoted by asking this research question?' Critical race research, for example, prioritizes research questions and methods which challenge racism and consider the power imbalance between the researcher and the researched (Thomas, 2009). Research which highlights the inequities and stereotyping of African American students in school may examine tests of achievement, but from a more emancipatory framework (Lynn, Yosso, Solorzano, & Parker, 2002).

Researchers or students do not always have a completely free choice of topic. Many may be working for, or supervised by, other researchers who have their own interests and agendas. This can raise questions for individuals' consciences, as the case study on my own 'taboo topic' in this chapter illustrates. Research questions are not 'neutral', but contain assumptions within them which can raise ethical questions. They also feed into political and social agendas. The ethically reflexive student considers these before proceeding. Participatory approaches often design research questions with the participant group themselves so that their framing of issues is inherent in the design from the start (Ennew & Beasley, 2006). This offers participants a voice within the design process, rather than simply being those who are passively 'studied' (Ennew & Beasley, 2006).

In Eva's project, she decided on a more participatory design process that draws together interested parties, such as those with cognitive decline and their advocates, to work in focus groups to identify how they wanted the study to be conducted and key questions to be asked. This includes external agencies (e.g. support groups or NGOs) as well as residents. It is important to note, however, that most IRBs/committees would require ethical permission before involving participants. For Eva, this negotiation took several months and she had to build this stage very explicitly into the design for review.

Quick question

Are there any topics or research questions you have come across that you consider unethical or would not want personally to study? Which ones and why?

RESEARCH DESIGN

Certain projects may be intrinsically unethical if their design clearly and obviously breaks one of the key principles of ethical research, such as social justice or beneficence. An example of this are projects which have a high probability of causing the participants significant and ongoing harm (even if they consented). I would classify most Nazi experimentation on humans in this category.

However, few research designs or questions are so obviously unethical. Rather, research designs often involve more subtle conflicts, for example, between the perceived benefit to science or society from increased knowledge vs. the potential distress of the subjects. In the introduction, I discussed Zimbardo's 'simulated prison camp' with participants given roles as guards and prisoners in the basement at Stanford. After the controversy, Zimbardo himself argued that the study design was not intrinsically unethical but that the study should have been monitored more carefully when running it to prevent bullying (Zimbardo, 1973). On the other hand, it was precisely the extreme behaviour in the absence of monitoring that led to the advancement of knowledge; the development of the social role theory of aggression. The experiment has been re-run with full ethics committee approval as a television programme (Reicher & Haslam, 2006; Zimbardo, 2006). However, the fact that it was by then a well-known experiment, and that it was being televised, may well have constrained participants behaviour. But did this experiment have to be run at all? An alternative approach would have been to use another method. For example, investigating how people take on the roles of victim (prisoners) and bully (guard) could have been done by following trainee prison guards and novice prisoners in an observation type study in real-life prisons.

For the researcher, therefore, ethical research design is about thinking through the implications of one's design before starting. There are several aspects to this. Firstly, the researcher needs to identify if any of the ethical principles/rules covered in Chapter 2 are brought into play within the initial design (e.g. is it a covert study, does it use vulnerable subjects, does it exclude certain types of participants, are there problems with anonymity or confidentiality, is the harm likely to be more than minimal?) If yes, they need to consider the justification for these choices (e.g. by the benefit to participants or to further knowledge). Secondly, the researcher needs to think through the choice of method, sampling and procedures in terms of ethical principles.

In Eva's project, there are a myriad of decisions about the design of the study which have ethical aspects. Should residents with memory difficulties participate, or just care workers as 'proxies' (i.e. people speaking for others)? How should consent procedures be conducted (e.g. once in written form, or verbally, or at the start of every encounter)? How would participants make their own wishes known, given possible difficulties with verbal communication? Is there some sense of obligation for participants to participate? Should participants be involved in the analysis and production of outputs and how would this work in practice for those with some cognitive decline? In Eva's case, she worked through each of these issues with her supervisor and an advisor from a support group, planning a study which was as potentially informative, but also respectful to participants as possible. She then presented these to the residents group and worked with them to finalize the design. One aspect of her design, relating to consent, was also changed by the ethics committee which required her to have formal training on how to assess the ability to consent.

Methods

Several issues concerning ethics are raised by methodological choices. One is whether all methods are equally ethical? It has been argued that qualitative methods have an inherently emancipatory function and pay a greater respect to human experience and the goals of social justice. As such, this is a criticism aimed at classic quantitative research in which the participant is viewed as a 'subject' who is the object of passive measurement and statistical manipulation. However, increasingly researchers are acknowledging the power of different methods to enact ethical goals. For example, statistical research by social epidemiologists has pointed powerfully to the continuing health inequalities between rich and poor in the same societies. This does not let statistical research off the ethical hook: the failure to measure certain variables, measure then in ways not consonant with people's self-identity or represent them in stereotyped ways indeed represent ethical transgressions. However, as Mertens and colleagues state 'methodologically, choices go beyond quantitative, qualitative or mixed methods to how to collect data about the reality of a concept in such a way that one feel confident that one has indeed captured that reality and done so in an ethical manner' (Mertens et al., 2009, p. 88). They use the example of researching issues in the deaf community using indigenous guidelines produced within the sign language community, publishing bilingually (in both print English and video-based sign) and sharing results with the community first, as examples of this in practice.

It is beyond the scope of this book to consider all of the ethical issues provoked by each method/type of data collection individually.

However, there are general guidelines, depending on whether the data is primary (collected by the researcher during the study) or secondary (uses existing data or archived material).

- Direct primary data methods with participants include surveys, experiments, quasi or natural experiments (e.g. conducted in everyday life), interviews and active participant observation/ethnography. As these methods involved direct contact between researcher and researched, they raise standard issues concerning informed consent (Chapter 7), privacy, anonymity and confidentiality (Chapter 8), and the risks/harm of the project (Chapter 9). If the research is with vulnerable groups/sensitive issues (Chapter 10) or children (Chapter 11), this raises additional issues. Other, often unpredictable issues can arise during data collection (Chapter 6).

- Indirect primary methods (e.g. passive observation, using existing Internet material) are typically less intrusive, which raises questions of whether there is an obligation to seek consent or make publically visible material anonymous (see Chapters 7 and 8, and on Internet research, Chapter 12).

- Deceptive or covert research, which compromises informed consent, remains ethically controversial (Chapter 7).

- Visual (video, photographic or drawing) methods raise typical consent issues, as well as additional ones concerning privacy and copyright (Chapter 7; also see Warren, 2002). Additionally anonymization may not be possible or desirable (Chapter 8).

- Research with groups and communities, such as researcher-created focus groups or interviewing couples or families, raises issues around how to ensure confidentiality and privacy within the group (Chapter 8), as well as the ethics around changing group dynamics through research.

- Case study research raises ethical issues over the feasibility and desirability of anonymity: about whether it is possible or desirable to hide the distinguishing features of the case (Chapter 8).

- Ethnographic methods in which the researcher lives within a culture or community over a significant time period raises issues concerning the explicitness and nature of consent (Chapter 7) as well as the management of research relationships over the longer term (Chapter 6) (see American Anthropological Association, 2004).

- Literature-based research (e.g. of media or literature reviews of research) does not have 'participants' in need of protection, but there are ethical issues concerning the fair and unbiased selection of sources and fair representation within the analysis.
- Secondary data analysis includes studying anonymized data sets, archive or publically available material. In general, the rule for ethical handling of archive or secondary data is that the original ethical basis on which the data was collected must be respected, as must be the rules of the archive or organization holding it. It is often exempt from full ethical review.

Another interesting issue is to consider whether there is an ethical rationale for encouraging the use of secondary data. It is tempting, for a researcher or student faced with creating an original piece of research, to want to collect one's own data set. However, in many instances, this is duplicating the efforts of others and may even represent a misuse of time spent, if similar existing data sets are not fully utilized. Secondary data analysis can also reveal new insights into existing material and facilitate the transparency of research. Many funding bodies, across different countries, also require researchers to archive their data for others to use (e.g. European Research Council, The Canadian Institutes of Health Research, the UK Economic and Social Research Council). This requires planning at the research design stage, such as building this into the consent process. There is further discussion of the ethics around reusing and storing secondary data in Chapter 8 in the section on data protection. Secondary data analysis is also often exempt from formal ethical review, for example, in the US it is exempt from the Common Rule if the data, documents or records are in the public domain or do not contain identifiers.

SAMPLING AND PAYMENT

Sampling

Who is included as participants (and who is excluded) is very much an ethical issue. Certain groups of participants go 'missing' from data for numerous reasons. They may be 'invisible' as a group to the researcher, for example, Sullivan (2009) points out that data on disability is often not collected, rendering data partial and skewed. Secondly, the population group from which the sample is drawn (randomly or purposively) may be very limited. Using white college students would be an example of this. Thirdly, some marginalized groups have less tradition of participating in research, may not see the point or may have active reasons for avoiding it (e.g. not wanting to give information to the 'authorities'.) Finally, as a researcher you may find it easier to ask 'people like yourself' to take part, say for an undergraduate project. For example, if you 'snowball sample' (asking one participant to recommend another) from a group of your own friends, you will probably end up with a sample very similar to yourself.

It is unethical to exclude certain groups for no good reason, as well as scientifically suspect. One way to tackle this is when you are designing your sample, ask yourself who might be excluded and is there any justification for this? You can then think of ways in which such biases could be rectified. For example, in a study on public attitudes towards new prenatal technologies I was conducting with my colleague, our first wave of participants were mainly women, Christians or not religious, and middle-class. Scientifically and morally, it did not make sense to consider this 'the public'. Furthermore, men are often excluded from research into prenatal decision-making. Our second wave of recruitment, therefore, asked specifically for men and religious/ethnic groups to participate (Farrimond & Kelly, 2011; Kelly & Farrimond, 2012).

Including vulnerable groups can also be practically difficult. However, the principle of social justice indicates it is fair to give the researched group themselves a voice. In Eva's project, a more inclusive sampling strategy involved including participants who were residents, some of whom had memory difficulties rather than simply asking proxies such as their relatives about their experiences. Although this was more time-consuming than just researching with relatives, this increased both the research quality (as it was more representative) and inclusivity.

Researching with people you know

It is relatively common, especially for those conducting a small-scale or student project, to recruit a 'convenience' sample from participants from those they know. Similarly, researching in a particular place or institution in which you already work or attend may seem ideal as a method of recruitment as you are already known and trusted. However, there are potential ethical issues. One is that the very thing that makes it easier to recruit participants, their knowledge and trust of you, also makes it harder for them to say no to participating, particularly if you ask them directly. You need to be sensitive to this, for example, by using a general advert displayed to everyone so those who are keen can come forward, or if you do approach individuals, be very clear that participation is voluntary. If the research is with a group or institution (e.g. a charity organization), then the participants' normal activities (e.g. attending prayer group on a Tuesday) shouldn't be disrupted; rather a separate group for research could be set up on another day. Secondly, it is much harder to anonymize a place or organization if you are a member of it. Just putting your affiliation on a publication (e.g. University of X), even if you have changed the organization's details in the text, can make it obvious that you are speaking from within the organization about that organization.

Finally, 'insider' data can be ethically more problematic to use given pre-existing relationships and associations, especially if your conclusions are controversial. This is particularly the case, for example, with action research in which the goal is to plan for and evaluate change within your own practice and/or institutional practices, a process which can get caught up in the local politics of the situation (Williamson & Prosser, 2002). Asking politically sensitive or difficult questions in an organization can leave the researcher vulnerable (e.g. in career terms), or simply unable to enact the desired changes. In Eva's project, issues arose when her recommendations for change in the care homes were seen as overly critical by those in charge, even though they had consented to participation.

Payment

Participants do not have to take part in research; it should be an entirely voluntary act. Clark (2010), in a small scale study, found there were three primary reasons for engaging with qualitative research: representation, political empowerment and informing change. Many participants hope that by taking part, they will be making a difference; essentially participating is akin to 'gift-giving' in this scenario. Participants can also find it hard to say no, which is why the 'right to withdraw' is so important.

One trickier ethical question is whether you should pay participants. There are two schools of thought. One is that in our economy, it is usual to pay people for their time. Not paying people for research represents 'taking advantage'. Another is that payment corrupts the voluntary nature of participation. Payment to participants is common in clinical and medical trials, to both clinicians and participants. My own view on payment is pragmatic rather than morally absolute. For example, I wanted to sample smokers for my PhD on smoking identities (Farrimond, Joffe, & Stenner, 2010). However, initially I didn't attract many smokers from low socio-economic groups (a well-known participant response bias), so I advertised in newspapers with a lower socio-economic status demographic, offering a voucher for a small amount. Although the amount was minimal, it attracted smokers from the desired group, who needed an additional 'rationale' to take part. I did not consider this unethical as it increased representation of the poorer group (social justice); the risk of participation was also very low, as was the sum paid. It would have been unethical if I had offered a large life-changing sum of money and the risk of participation very high. In Eva's project, there was much keenness amongst most residents to take part to have their say about their experiences and offering payment was not considered appropriate.

ANALYSIS AND DISSEMINATION

Data analysis

It is important that when you analyse data, that your results are first and foremost valid and sound; that your results have integrity stemming from your own integrity, if you like. In many ways, the issue of how to ensure quality in data analysis in both qualitative and quantitative (and mixed) analysis is an ethical one. If your data does not represent the phenomenon under study, has missing data or 'voices', excludes relevant data, comes to the wrong conclusion due to mis-analysis or is not transparently conducted (so that others can see what you have done), then it does not have integrity and is scientifically suspect. It may also represent a waste of public funds. In quantitative research, quality is ensured through reliability (consistency of measurement) and validity (extent to which the phenomenon claimed to be measured has actually been measured in the study) (e.g. Coolican, 2009; Patten, 2002). Quality criterion for qualitative research has been debated, but includes transparency, examining counter-evidence/deviant cases, replicating coding and using data triangulation amongst others (e.g. Cohen & Crabtree, 2008; Flick, 2006). It is ethical to do research to the highest possible standard; to this end, it is worth reading some of the quality criteria literature or quality guidelines provided by journals.

To take an example, ethical analysis should include all of the relevant data (i.e. fairly represent the phenomenon under study). There have been numerous discussions about practices of 'data fishing' (e.g. looking for any associations rather than theorized ones) and the manipulation of data in statistical analyses (e.g. the excluding of relevant data as 'outliners' or cutting the data numerous ways to achieve a significant result). This is not a trivial issue. If a set of experiments is conducted that indicate a certain educational program is beneficial, it may be adopted. If there is a deliberate manipulation of the data, then the incorrect result may inform policy and lead children's educations to change in non-beneficial ways (Mark & Gamble, 2009). Similarly, in qualitative research, there can be a temptation to include a 'juicy quote', which may not represent the position of the majority of the interviewees. Doing data analysis with integrity means representing the data fully, including (but not over-representing) outliers or exceptional cases.

Within qualitative designs, particularly participatory approaches, doing data analysis with integrity may also include involving the participants themselves in the analysis (Ennew & Beasley, 2006). This can involve returning interview transcripts for participant comments, or 'member checking' where participants check back on their own data to see if they agree with the interpretation. Participants may also review articles or reports before publication. This model of co-production is a response to the exclusion of participants and their social worlds. For example, little research till the 1990s about disability involved disabled people or considered disability in terms of social discrimination rather than personal experience (Oliver, 1992). However, the researcher may want to maintain control over certain aspects of the research process even within a broadly participatory model (Shakespeare, 1997). In Eva's project, she conducted an initial analysis herself, which she then presented to a selection of residents for their feedback. However, she found few were willing to challenge her interpretation but rather sought to reassure her she'd 'done a good job'. It was unclear whether this reflected the ongoing power relationship especially with vulnerable groups or was linked with possible cognitive decline.

Reporting your data with integrity is not the same as avoiding misconduct, which refers to practices such as falsifying data or falsifying records or materials (see below). However, many ethics codes (e.g. APA) recommend retaining your primary data for five years and making it available for reanalysis for reasons of transparency and fraud prevention.

Dissemination and impact

Do you have a duty to share your results and with whom? It has been argued recently that researchers do have a moral obligation to make their results accessible to those that fund them or take part in the research. Public dissemination can take place through multiple channels, such as interactive media, podcasts or simply placing a copy of the findings (not published) on a website. Institutional repositories are also increasingly common, where work within the university is placed for open access after checks with the publishers have taken place to determine copyright. It has been argued that online open access journals also provide a more ethical publication route for funded research rather than exclusive paper/online journals, which are expensive and only accessible within institutions. Opportunities for public engagement may also present themselves, such as presenting at public social science events or open evenings.

The moral duty to share one's results has to be balanced against the need to protect one's intellectual property (e.g. by publishing work or placing a copyright symbol on it asserting one's authorship before widespread dissemination). In participatory research, participants themselves may engage in dissemination activities (e.g. narrating their stories).

Impact refers to the influence that a particular piece of research has over the short and longer term. This could mean direct influence in the context in which the research took place (e.g. the individual school or organization) or more indirect, through policy routes (e.g. forming part of a body of evidence resulting in policy change). In participatory or transformative research, the change agenda is built in. There is clearly a strong ethical imperative to maximize the impact of conducted research; making it count, if you like. However, tricky ethical issues can arise. One is the management of expectations for participants about change. It may be very frustrating if people participate on the basis of change, but it is not forthcoming, perhaps due to entrenched political positions. Furthermore, as Khanlou and Peter argue, in a review of the ethical issues presented by participatory action research, the very act of challenging the status quo may leave a community more vulnerable and exposed in a hostile environment (Khanlou & Peter, 2005). In other words, positive social impact cannot be presumed, but needs careful and intentional management.

Occasionally, organizations or funders may be so concerned about their reputation at the point of dissemination, they threaten to withdraw consent, try to prevent publication or insist on pre-screening before publication. If this infringes on your academic freedom, seek legal and ethical advice from your institution.

Eva's project had a social justice/change agenda, in that she was motivated to analyse the needs of residents in care homes to provide recommendations, at both the local and policy level. Indeed, the owners of the care homes had consented to give access to their residents and homes on the basis that she would write a report analysing the residents' needs. However, the owners were unprepared for the critical nature of the report and started to worry her research may reflect badly on them. Ultimately, she was able to negotiate this sensitively by emphasizing the practicality of the solutions developed with participants, and reassuring them about the high level of anonymity she would provide in publication. In hindsight, she wished she had involved the management more collaboratively in the research process from the outset, rather than viewing them as gatekeepers to access the 'real' (i.e. residents) participants.

AUTHORSHIP, MISCONDUCT AND FRAUD

Authorship

Authorship, or who gets their name on a paper or report, remains, in my view, an ethically fraught area. Normative practices which are ethically questionable include: including as authors people who have not made a substantial contribution to the paper because it was 'expected', because they were a major funder, or because they were well-known and it was hoped their inclusion would make the paper more publishable (e.g. ghost authorship). In the Andrew Wakefield case concerning the MMR vaccination and autism, it was revealed that one of the original authors cited on the 1998 paper had not seen the final version and was found guilty of misconduct as a consequence (Godlee, Smith, & Marcovitch, 2011). More common, however, are cases where faculty staff are unjustifiably given (or give themselves) most senior authorship (first or last depending on the discipline) and the contribution of the main writer, such as the student, is devalued. As well as intellectually dishonest, this is extremely problematic for postgraduates who rely on authoring publications to establish their research careers.

The APA's 2002 Ethics Code (Standard 8.12) states, 'faculty advisors should discuss publication credit with students as early as feasible and throughout the research and publication process as appropriate.' An upfront conversation about authorship needs to be had before writing anything for external publication. It can be quite embarrassing to do so, but personally now I never write anything without having explicitly agreed the order of authors before I start. It also helps to have a frank conversation about how to divide up the data, so that people do not duplicate efforts. This discussion is necessary given the continuing hierarchical relationship between students/assistants and faculty staff. Both disciplinary ethics codes and authorship guidelines for journals contain information on authorship: if a conflict arises, consult these before making your case.

Misconduct and fraud

Misconduct is often referred to as FFP: Fabrication, Falsification and Plagiarism, although the definitions of these remain controversial. Shamoo and Resnick provide a comprehensive review of the history of scientific misconduct, arguing that by the time misconduct is detected and dealt with at an institutional or legal level, it is likely to represent only the 'tip of the iceberg' of unethical practices (Shamoo & Resnick, 2009, pp. 93–118). Recent examples include a German Defence Minister who was stripped of his PhD on constitutional treaties in the EU when it was found that more than half of it was identical to other sources (http://www.bbc.co.uk/news/world-europe-12566502, Accessed, 16/9/2012). The Office of Research Integrity in the US functions to make recommendations and sanction publically funded instances of fraud or misconduct (e.g. for National Institute of Health grants; Shamoo & Resnick, 2009). Fraud and misconduct is also investigated by institutions, journals and professional bodies who usually have disciplinary committees.

It is unclear how much social research is tainted by fraud or misconduct as there have been fewer high-profile cases than in medicine and science. In qualitative research, for example, there may be less motivation to falsify data as the problem of getting a null result is less pressing. Common problems include: not having completed enough data (so making up a portion of it) or not being overly truthful to get participants (e.g. withholding the source of funding). As to what motivates people to commit fraud or misconduct, LaFolette points out a number of factors: from 'human failings' to a system in which the 'slippery slope' seemed the only route to success (e.g. pressure to publish or get grants; LaFolette, 1994).

Plagiarism is a problem in all disciplines. Plagiarism means to copy someone else's ideas without acknowledgement (e.g. with no reference). For a review of current literature on plagarism, see Park (2003). One problem, exacerbated by the Internet era in which multiple texts on pretty much any topic are available, is that some students do not appear to understand what constitutes plagiarism. Many cut and paste large chunks from the Internet, use existing text without acknowledgement or even pay others to do their papers (or download 'off-the-shelf' ones), but are still surprised when confronted with accusations of plagiarism. Institutions take plagiarism very seriously, and will request all students to read their plagiarism policy; they may also run student work through plagiarism software. I also have experience of faculty staff 'borrowing' ideas from meetings or confidential documents from other researchers and presenting them as their own in journals or grant proposals.

Plagiarism is a form of stealing and harms academic integrity greatly (see also Authorship in this section). However, reporting someone for misconduct or plagiarism is an ethical decision as it may have severe consequences for their qualification or career. If the instance is debatable (e.g. not clearly plagiarism), I would discuss it hypothetically or in confidence first with a supervisor/senior staff member. Many institutions also have an Academic Misconduct Officer to consult.

FUNDING/CONFLICTS OF INTEREST

Many people think of a 'conflict of interest' in big terms, for example, having funding from a problematic source such as a company or organization which has aims not compatible with genuine academic freedom (e.g. if a government paid you to evaluate how great their education program was and didn't want to hear any negative outcomes). This is not necessarily the case. It is becoming more common to involve social scientists, lawyers and bioethicists in developing products or offering research services to the market, such as in pharmaceuticals or new technologies (e.g. as advisors, submitting patents). This of itself is not necessarily problematic, unless it is not declared or is hidden in some way. The Missenden Code (cited in the Appendix) outlines the ideal ethical relationship between commercial companies, universities and their employees in the UK.

So, to whom do you need to declare your funding source and any conflict of interest? Certainly journal editors and funding bodies expect full disclosure of any relevant details. Ethical researchers lie on the generous side of interpreting a 'conflict of interest', preferring to declare anything mildly relevant and allowing the audience to judge.

Do your research participants have a 'right to know' where your funding is obtained? In most cases, I would argue yes, it is part of informed consent. They may or may not wish to participate if they know the source of funding, for example, if they have a principled objection to taking part in research funded by particular religious or political groups. The exception to this may be if a researcher is working covertly, either to access an otherwise hidden but scientifically important phenomenon, or for their own safety (see Hot Topic: Informed Consent (Chapter 7)).

IS BADLY DESIGNED RESEARCH UNETHICAL?

It has been argued that 'unethical science is bad science'. However, as the debate over whether to use the possibly informative, but horrifically obtained results of Nazi experimentation has shown, this is not always the case (Ziporyn, 1990). Indeed, where controversy over the ethics of social science studies has attracted attention in the literature, it is usually because the research is both profoundly informative in terms of social knowledge, but ethically problematic. Ethically suspect research that tells us nothing has little impact.

Hammersley has argued that an over-preoccupation with ethics, which he terms 'ethicism' has led to a neglect of research techniques in qualitative research (Hammersley, 1999). I agree that certain practices such participants reviewing transcripts or including their input in analysis/writing have become a little formulaic as ways of 'being ethical'. If the resulting analysis is poor (e.g. rests at a descriptive level), then you have wasted everyone's time (and money) including the participants. To this extent, I would argue, improving research quality is an ethical act. Furthermore, the aim of this chapter has not been to set out a list of research designs which are more inherently ethical than others, but rather to show how ethical issues are embedded within the 'lifecycle' of research projects.

75

Often, 'poor design' is really poorly executed design. This may have ethical implications. A covert study in which the researcher does not initially reveal their identity to reveal some 'greater good' such as the hypocrisy of a political organization may be ethically justified. But if the execution of the design is poor, for example, the targets of their attention are wrongly chosen or the participants not given the right to reply, then the authenticity and robustness of the study may be fatally compromised. Similarly, a standard semi-structured interview may be a seemingly ethically sound choice to give voice to the narratives of prisoners facing trial. However, if the researcher, perhaps though inexperience, plans far too many interviews and none are analysed in depth, the potential ethical impact of the research is compromised.

Despite agreeing that poor design may have ethical implications, however, I disagree with the tendency of IRBs or ethics committees to interfere greatly with research design unless there are clear ethical breaches. It is not clear from examining research protocols what the value of a given project will really be in five years time. I have seen extremely unpromising PhD proposals turn in four years into beautifully researched and socially valuable projects. Equally, experienced researchers sometimes 'talk the talk' around inflating the likely impact of their work. Unless the project shows such an inadequate understanding of design it suggests incompetence, or directly transgresses ethical principles, then I think IRBs/committees should focus on avoiding harms and not on optimizing designs.

SUMMARY

This chapter has considered how ethical issues and dilemmas are raised throughout the 'lifecycle' of a research project, from choosing which research questions to ask, to doing data analysis which has integrity. Having chosen a research design, the next step in the ethical 'lifecycle' of a project is to undergo ethical review of the proposal. The next chapter looks at how to make good ethics applications and gain institutional approval.

CASE STUDY: 'NORMALS AND NON-NORMALS' – A TOPIC TOO FAR?

As a junior level researcher, I was asked to participate in a research project auditing pre-natal choices in the health care system. When I read the project description, I noticed language concerning 'normals' (non-Down Syndrome foetuses) and 'non-normals' (Down Syndrome foetuses) in the flowcharts. When I looked at the goals of the project, they were framed as making the prenatal testing process more 'efficient' and 'improving outcomes'. I felt that terminating more 'non-normals' was the tacit motivation behind the audit. I felt uncomfortable with the framing of the research, in either the language or the goals, so I told the project team I didn't want to participate. I do not have any principled objection to social science research into prenatal testing per se, and a few years later, conducted a study with a colleague looking at public attitudes towards new forms of prenatal testing (Farrimond & Kelly, 2011; Kelly & Farrimond, 2012). However, this second study did not create the same sense of ambivalence, as I felt it allowed participants their voice, including those speaking from a disability rights perspective and those pro-expansion of testing. Refusing to participate on the initial project was presented as a lost opportunity for funding by the project organizers, one of whom got very angry at the implication their audit was not neutral but discriminatory. My immediate managers were accepting of the decision. I was also prepared to make a financial sacrifice, of a half-day's salary a week not to participate. This experience crystallized to me that it is perfectly legitimate to want to direct your energy towards research you believe personally to be ethical and valuable in terms of its goals (or at least doesn't keep you awake at night).

Ethical Dilemma 4: Whose idea was it?

Peter has always believed that it is important to share ideas and work collaboratively with his colleagues. He was about to submit his PhD, when he was approached by an interested researcher from another country who also shared his passion for the anthropology of political action. In the context of a long email discussion about having similar ideas and meeting at the next conference, he was asked if he would mind sharing the final chapter of his thesis on a totally confidential basis. He did so and thought nothing of it, until six months later, having submitted his thesis, he was asked to review a grant application. On reading it, he realized that the design for the study was identical to the one proposed in his conclusions chapter, down to the choice of design, participants, even the location for fieldwork. He now feels very naïve, but when he approached his departmental head, they seemed uninterested in pursuing the matter further.

1. What should Peter do next?
2. What steps could Peter take in the future to ensure his work is protected as intellectual property, but that he can share it with others?
3. Have you experienced either people falsifying data, plagiarizing or stealing ideas? What happened? What do you think should change, if anything, to the current system of detecting and deterring misconduct?

5 Writing a Successful Ethics Proposal

This chapter is not just for those who are making an ethics application to an IRB or ethics committee, but for anyone doing a written project that involves ethics review. I have read over 250 of these types of applications (as well as having written a few of my own). I have noticed that applicants make similar mistakes time and again. These are not necessarily serious failures, but lead to delays, requests for clarification, more amendments, or in the worst case, may lead the panel to question the ethical competence of the applicant.

This chapter aims to save you that experience, by identifying five of the most common problems with written ethics applications and telling you how to solve them. It also covers what to do before and after the decision on your application is made. I do not claim speak for all committee or IRB members. Every one may have their own 'pet hates' in terms of problem applications. The key point, however, is that they are there to review the ethics of the project. If they get bogged down with a poorly written and presented application, ethics review is made all the harder.

Example: Brian's Study

Brian wants to conduct a small-scale qualitative study of the experience of bankruptcy amongst owners and directors of small/medium size businesses since 2009. He himself is a mature student who went bankrupt in this time period, so is not experienced with IRBs/ethics committees or their forms. His departmental administrator has advised him that he needs to submit an ethics application well in advance of any planned data collection.

BEFORE MAKING AN APPLICATION

Finding out what is required

Chapter 3 detailed the typical structure and processes of Institutional Review Boards (IRBs) and ethics committees. The next step is to find out the specific requirements for ethics review in your institution or workplace, for your particular project, assignment or paper. Although this sounds rather obvious, students or staff are sometimes unsure what to do or get caught out by changes in procedures. Furthermore, ethics review requirements vary considerably, depending on type, discipline and the institution. Institutions do not, in general, give 'retrospective' ethics permission for research already conducted. If you have already been collecting data, you are unlikely to get permission to use it. As Chapter 1 showed, failure to secure ethics approval may have serious consequences (e.g. may jeopardize your PhD or mean the work is not publishable).

Institutions or workplaces place their ethics review procedures, forms and guidelines on the Internet or in student/staff handbooks. In health institutions (National Institutes of Health (NIH) and National Health Service (NHS)), these procedures are detailed at length on their relevant websites. Read the guidelines before you start, as they usually contain very clear instructions on how to fill in each section of the form.

It is also important to pay attention to the timeline of ethical review in your institution. Do not assume ethical review will be straightforward and timely; it may be neither. Many committees/IRBs sit only a few times a year. This means planning well in advance. For example, I find many committees/IRBs don't sit in the summer months, so for a research study starting in September, you may need to submit an application back in May/June. A light-touch system may take less time. It's better to check this at the start of the year so as not to get caught out (as I have been at least once).

As mentioned in Chapter 3, there will be a designated person to assist with the administrative side of ethics review. This might be the departmental administrator within a university or the secretary of the IRB/committee. It is well worth getting in touch with them and briefly clarifying the procedures and timeframe. If you are researching on a contentious topic (e.g. terrorism, sexuality, drug use in minors) or method (e.g. covert research), or are just unsure how a particular case might be handled (e.g. consent with under 18's), you might also approach the Chair of the IRB/committee to ask for informal advice before submitting an application. Review decisions are based on local precedents, so it makes sense to write your application keeping them in mind (Stark & Hedgecoe, 2010).

Planning your writing

Most forms are pretty standard in their format. There is a section or 'protocol' to inform the review panel about your project, the research goals and the methodology. The protocol is important as it has to be an accurate statement of what you intend to do in the project; if the protocol is subsequently changed after review (e.g. you interview a different group using a different schedule), then your project won't be covered (Sieber, 2000). Other sections ask for information on the ethical issues raised by your project and how these will be managed. These typically include informed consent, anonymity/confidentiality, assessment of possible harms/benefits, data protection, conflict of interest and possibly insurance. The application may require relevant supporting documents to be attached, such as a sample consent form or any instruments you are using (e.g. questionnaires/interview schedule). It may require institutional signatories (e.g. supervisor, head of faculty, ethics officer). Minimal risk applications often ask for a brief description and to tick boxes to confirm that the research does not fall into a list of 'higher risk' categories.

It is difficult to dash off an ethics application or project quickly unless you have written many before. Like all written work, it will benefit from good advice from others, and a careful proof-read. The first step is to create a rough draft. For each section (e.g. consent), read the appropriate sections in this book or discuss with a relevant person, then write in simple terms how this ethical issue is approached in your research. Do not just identify ethical issues; explain how they are going to be managed. Then, check your draft against the five common problems described in this chapter and make further changes. Finally, see if you can find a more experienced researcher, the ethics officer or a supervisor to read it through before submitting it for assessment. Many institutions require ethics forms to be signed off by staff before it goes to any board or committee as a quality control measure.

Problem 1: Not enough detail or poorly written project explanation

Solution: Provide a concise but detailed explanation of your project suitable for non-experts to read

This section should be concise but detailed enough for the committee or board to understand (a) the theoretical and practical rationale for undertaking this project, (b) the project aims, (c) the methodological design and (d) the specific procedures to be followed. Often students, and even staff, simply copy their description of the project from elsewhere, such as a grant application. This is not necessarily a good idea. Committees and IRBs may not know much about your particular specialization or topic area. The explanation of the project should therefore be written in a way that reasonably intelligent but non-expert people can understand it. Some ethics review boards require you to attach any grant application or proposal separately, and then provide a short lay explanation on the form. Again, the emphasis is on clear, concise explanation.

Methods sections in which you explain your design and procedures are also vital to get right. A committee/IRB simply cannot review a project if they are not sure what is actually going to happen. Provide a couple of lines on the rationale for choosing your method but concentrate your explanation on the procedure. Firstly, explain who will constitute your sample. Specify where you are recruiting (e.g. the country, the specific town/village or specific locations such as businesses, institutions, family members, anyone who is passing by the university on a Friday afternoon) and who you are recruiting (e.g. older people between the ages of 65 and 75, under 18's, people from a certain ethnic group, any member of a given church). Also explain how they will be recruited (e.g. adverts placed on notice boards, contacted through an open email, from a doctor's list). In some review procedures, you will need to include the invitation letter or advert. You then need to explain what will happen to participants from that point of first contact.

The aim is to provide a detailed explanation of what it will be like to be a participant in your particular study, so that the ethics of participating can be evaluated. Here's an example short methods section for Brian's bankruptcy study (full review of a substantial project may require more detail).

Example: Short methods section

My study 'The experience of bankruptcy amongst business people in rural areas in the 2008–current recession' uses an interview design. My sample will be business people who run small-to-medium enterprises (up to 500 employees) in the rural southern regions. I will interview 20 managers and directors of business. I will recruit people by advertising through local business organizations. I enclose a copy of my advert with this application. The advert asks business people if they would like to participate, and gives them my contact details at the university. Once they respond, I will give them more details by email. Once they have agreed to participate, I will then liaise with them to find a suitable time and location for the first interview, preferably their business premises or at the university if they are prepared to travel. I will offer travel expenses. Once a time has been arranged, I will conduct a semi-structured interview with the participant taking approximately an hour. The interview schedule is included with this application. I will arrange the second interview at the end of the first. Afterwards, I will email participants to thank them and provide them with a copy of their transcript asking if they want to amend it.

Problem 2: Poor assessment of risk/harm

Solution: Balanced and reasonable assessment, including benefits as well as harms

I find that applicants often make one of two opposing mistakes with assessment of possible risks/harms. One is to deny there is likely to be any harm whatsoever from taking part in their study. What they often mean is that the harms are likely to be 'minimal or low risk' but have not clarified this. Unfortunately it is not always low-risk projects which are marked 'Not Applicable' in the 'risks' section;

I have spotted major researcher safety or covert designs marked as 'low risk'. Other applicants go to the other extreme and exaggerate the likely harms. An example of this would be for a student to suggest offering counselling for dealing with distress during an interview study about a relatively usual topic (e.g. health) to deal with the 'trauma' of any interview. If the interview is likely to be very traumatic, then it may not be sensible to conduct it as student research at all; it is also impractical to offer counselling for all qualitative studies. A more nuanced approach is one which takes a common sense view on 'harms' to participants.

The important thing to note is that within research ethics, 'minimal risk' or 'harms' has a specific meaning. Definitions of 'harm' take into account two parameters. One is whether this is a risk or harm participants would encounter in their everyday life. Being observed by others, or talking about a distressing time in your life, or even putting your hand in cold water for 10 seconds might be a bit unpleasant, but they are not wholly outside our normal everyday experiences, and if people are warned about what will happen in advance and know they can stop at any time, it does not seem unreasonable to ask them to do these things. The second is the duration of any risk or harm. If a qualitative interview covers sexual abuse in childhood or traumatic memories, it is reasonable to consider this may have longer lasting detrimental impact. Offering counselling or working with an established organization to support participants during research would represent a sensible way of managing potential harm for this topic. Similarly, if a psychologist conducts an experiment which temporarily disorients participants who then perform a series of cognitive tests, the onus is on the researcher to take care of the participants until the effects have worn off or reverse the effects with another procedure.

Risks or harms can be broadly classified as follows: (a) physical or psychological harms, (b) financial, social or reputational harms and (c) researcher safety. Many applications fail to consider the latter in particular; lone research, research into particular topics or with some marginalized groups, or in less safe countries can all pose a risk to the researcher.

If you are having difficulty with assessing the harms and benefits of your project, read the Hot Topic 'Assessment of Possible Harms' in

Chapter 9. Think carefully about what it would be like to be a participant in this study and about some of the possible (i.e. quite likely rather than very improbable) outcomes for them. Think about the level of the harm in terms of being usual or long-lasting. Once you have identified the appropriate 'harms' for your project, you then need to explain clearly in your application how you are minimizing these and conducting appropriate risk management.

Example: Assessment of possible harms

In my project interviewing business people who have recently gone bankrupt in the recession, there are several possible harms. Firstly, it is important to maintain confidentiality between individuals and between companies, particularly with sensitive business information. I will ensure that I maintain privacy and confidentiality consciously at all times. A second harm might be to the reputation of the business person in the wider world. I will ensure not only that their names are made anonymous, but other identifying information (e.g. job title, name of organization) is changed in discussion with them. A final harm might be that this topic is distressing to the interviewees. I shall handle this sensitively if they get upset or distressed, by asking them if they would like to pause the interview or for me to switch the tape off (and listen to them meanwhile). I will also remind them that they can stop at any time. My information sheet contains details of organizations that can further advice business people about financial and emotional matters relating to bankruptcy.

It is also important to stress the benefits of your research, both to participants themselves, and in the ethics application. If you constantly talk about harms, it implies that research is a risky business with no upside. This is not the case. Conducting research is a valuable social enterprise and individuals who participate may well get something out of it. There is nothing wrong with pointing this out.

Example: Benefits to participation

Some participants may find talking about their experiences of recent bankruptcy to be a therapeutic experience. They may also be motivated to help others by provide insight about the needs of those

85

facing bankruptcy; providing an analysis of the nature of desired support is one of the aims of this research project.

Problem 3: Unrealistic suggestions

Solution: Only include what you are actually going to do and what is really necessary

One intrinsic flaw in ethics review which has been noted by numerous commentators is that it is essentially a set of promises about what you will do. Rarely is there any compliance procedure afterwards to check if you did what you said. For this reason, it is tempting for inexperienced researchers, students or staff, to include practices which they are not intending to carry out. However, your ethics form should not be a work of fiction. Furthermore, experienced ethics reviewers may well spot the impracticality of some suggestions, which may lead them to doubt the competence of the researcher.

Examples include a student who claimed that the area he was researching in was hostile to certain political groups, so that he would need to use oral consent and carry no names or addresses, then faithfully detailed how he would contact the participants to review their transcripts and send them a copy of the study report. Either it is too dangerous to hold names on paper or it isn't. Such claims undermine faith of the board/committee that this researcher has a good understanding of the risks facing them and are not, sadly, uncommon.

Similarly, if you are having participants take part in a one-off interview or survey, then just state this. Saying participants are involved in the research design, or that you will send transcripts or PhD thesis to them for review, should only be included if you are genuinely doing these things, not to make the project 'look good' or to fill the section on the form about 'participant feedback'. I always raise a small smile anyway when applicants say they will send out 40 PhD theses to their participants, as it would be totally impractical and expensive. Directing them towards a website or library holding the thesis, or producing a one-page tailored report for them, is much more practical and honest.

Another common promise I see increasingly is that at the end of the research process, the researcher will check with the participant before any of their quotes are used in publications. To me, this seems like over-egging the ethical pudding. There is certainly a case for involving participants in analysis and publication in a participatory model. But many people who claim to check back are not using participatory models and have already sought consent for use of quotes once in the original consent form. Furthermore, it is doubtful if many do actually check; it is time-consuming if there are 40 interviewees and multiple papers. There may be exceptions where returning to participants is a good idea; if engaged in proper participatory models or if there are issues of reputation for public figures and you wish to re-check a potentially controversial quote. However, my feeling is that for many, this is another fantasy claim.

In short, say what you are going to do and don't claim to be doing things that you are not. If you are going to use oral consent, say so and justify it. If you are not going to be in ongoing contact with your participants after the study, say so and reflect on this. The practice of embellishment is partly the fault of ethics IRBs and committees that often seek formulaic answers within set sections of the form. However, there is also an onus on the researcher to be as honest as possible.

Example: Participant involvement

Participants will be interviewed twice by the applicant over a three-month period. A pilot interview will be tested with a small sample and suggestions from participants incorporated. Participants will be sent their own transcripts for review. Participants will not be involved in the analysis or writing of papers. A short one-page report will be sent to participants by email at the end of the study detailing the main findings.

Problem 4: Failure to use or creatively adapt 'standard' materials

Solution: Adapt what exists to the needs of your participants

Many ethics review procedures have sample copies of the type of materials you might need, such as consent forms, information sheets and adverts for participants. If they already exist, it makes sense to use them as a solid basis for your own, as they usually cover the key points with which the committee/IRB will be concerned, such as anonymity, informed consent, any legal phrases and so on. There is no point reinventing the wheel if your project is straightforward.

However, there can be a big advantage in adapting these standardized materials to meet the needs of your participants. Not all sample consent forms are appropriate for all participant groups. If you are researching with a vulnerable group, then tailoring the material will be required. For example, if you are researching with adults with cognitive difficulties or younger children, then you may want to change the form to use simpler phrases and perhaps symbols or pictures which they could point to, to indicate consent, or use Makaton (a type of sign language) if they commonly use this. Easy Read formats can also be used which are accessible to those who have issues with literacy (websites and study materials can be 'translated' using these). Consent forms and information sheets should also be understandable by the target population. A common rule of thumb is to aim the level of writing at that which an 11- or 12-year-old could read and understand. This is simpler than most consent forms and information sheets you see. In short, avoid obvious errors and omissions by using pre-prepared materials, but also consider adapting them to the needs of your research population. For more on how to ensure informed consent, see Chapter 7.

Example: Informed consent

Participants will be given a separate information sheet and consent form. Participants will sign two copies of a written consent form, one for them to keep and one to be retained by the researcher. It will inform them that the interviews will be anonymous (i.e. with their name and any identifying details of their company altered in discussion with them) and confidential (discussed only with my supervisor). I will also let them know that ideally we will do two interviews, three months apart, when they first make contact by email or phone.

Problem 5: Ethical 'hypersensitivity'

Solution: Keep a perspective about ethical review

The main problem most IRBs/committees see is a failure to grasp even quite basic ethical principles or a lack of knowledge of standard ethical practices. So, ethical 'hypersensitivity' is only a problem for a minority, but a very real one. Some researchers or students, having never really thought about research ethics before attending a research ethics class, sometimes become hypersensitive to ethical issues in their research, to the extent that they start excessively worrying about them or changing their design to meet imagined ethical issues. One student who attended a workshop of mine suddenly became concerned about ethical issues in her study on religious practices abroad. She sought advice from three senior professors, the Ethics Chair, had in place every risk management strategy possible, but was still worried about proceeding. I was able to reassure her that if the weight of opinion of very senior staff was that this project was both ethical and sensible, then she should go ahead, which she did. Hammersley (1999) has written about 'ethicism', or a tendency to value research not by its quality, but by the extent to which it is perceived to embody ethical values. Ethical 'hypersensitivity' represents the personal level experience of this structural level preoccupation with ethics.

Ethical 'hypersensitivity' is also evidenced when researchers get so worried that their project will not meet ethical review standards, they either abandon it or change it dramatically beforehand. Some of the most important social science and scientific work is the most ethically problematic. Again, responsibility rests firmly with IRBs/committees to not be too risk-averse. Risky projects where the researcher displays poor ethical competence are always likely to attract amendments or even be vetoed. However, my experience is that even very inherently problematic research (e.g. with prisoners, sex offenders, in risky regions of the world) is far more likely to get ethical approval if the team or individual shows high ethical competence in their application. As stated previously, if serious problems are anticipated or you even just want clarification of the usual protocol, then ask for discussion of the project with the Chair/committee representatives before submission. I have had such discussions myself several times and frequently see staff and students for pre-submission meetings.

Example: Seeking advice

Brian was worried that the committee may have issues with possible distress for interviewees talking about bankruptcy, covering issues such as losing their livelihoods, homes as well the impact in their personal lives. After speaking with the ethics rep for his discipline, he decided to include sources of further support in the information sheet, as well as a detailed explanation of how he would handle distress in an interview situation.

AFTER A DECISION

Making amendments

After submission and the committee has met, a decision is issued, usually within a specified timeframe. If it is a light touch or expedited review, or an internal departmental procedure, you may simply receive an immediate approval and signature and the process is finished, unless it is decided the project requires full review. If your project has gone to full review, there are several outcomes. In the best case scenario you are given approval without any amendments and a certificate is issued. More likely, IRBs or committees require amendments to the proposal, which they will specify and need to be completed within a short amount of time. These should be made quickly and thoroughly so as to speed up the process of approval. The worst-case scenario is that the project is rejected by the IRB/committee in its current form. In this instance, I would contact the Chair/departmental representative to see how to proceed.

Example: Amendments

Brian submitted his ethics proposal and received an email reply within two weeks of the meeting. The project was approved with a couple of small amendments, one being to send the information sheet in advance so that participants could consider the topic before the interview date. The other related to clarifying the precise details of data storage. Although slightly disgruntled at what seemed like minor points, Brian immediately amended the proposal, filed his certificate and started data collection shortly afterwards.

What if you disagree with the decision?

If the amendment or decision you disagree with is relatively minor, such as in the example above, I would just make the change. Challenges to committee decisions are relatively rare, but could be considered if you believe that the amendments suggested by the IRB/committee significantly alter the project aims or procedure in a way that compromises the project, or if you fundamentally disagree with their interpretation of ethical principles. IRBs/committees should have an appeals/complaints procedure. If it is not on their website or in their literature, ask the IRB/committee administrator. You may just be asked to put your objection in writing to the Chair or submit the proposal for re-review.

I personally think that a well-argued rebuttal of a committee's decision is justified on (rare) occasions. Many decisions, for example, over anonymity in Internet research or the use of oral consent are a matter of debate and consensus, and there is no 'right answer' in every situation. IRBs/committees are simply researchers or people with expertise who sit in a room together and agree on a decision on a given day. Their decisions are not infallible, nor should they be engraved in stone. Challenging the authority of an IRB/committee decision should not be done just for the sake of it. It may not end in your favour. However, if you have a strong and justifiable reason for making a challenge, make your appeal in writing, ideally citing relevant codes and/or examples of similar designs in the literature.

Keeping ethics documents secure

This again sounds very obvious, but it is important to store the project approval document carefully. It may be needed for evidence of ethical review in a thesis or researching abroad or for insurance purposes. Don't depend on the committee/IRB to keep a copy, they may move offices, change their structure or disband and reform.

One option is to create a file called 'Ethics for X project' containing the application, printouts of any email discussions or amendments, the certificate, and also provides somewhere to keep consent forms and any other correspondence. I needed to show a seven-year-old certificate for my PhD thesis defence, as well as examples of consent forms. The material was not easily accessible, as I had moved institutions twice, so I have learnt the hard way how important it is to file ethics papers properly. Ethical audits are increasingly common from funding agencies or institutions (e.g. NHS in the UK). Systematic and secure document storage is vital in case of audits or future use.

Ethical competence

When thinking how to summarize this section, I realized that what most ethics committee/IRB members are looking for is 'ethical competence'. By ethical competence, I mean the ability to identify and think through the ethical dilemmas presented by their particular project, in the light of ethical principles and legal issues. It is not that IRBs/committees think the form itself is the be all and end all of ethics. Rather, the form represents a snapshot of the applicant's 'ethical competence' at a particular time.

It is, of course, possible that a candidate is highly ethically competent, but fails to transmit that on the form. This is not, in my view, often the case. On the very rare occasions when the committee I sit on has returned a poor or rejected application, it is clear that the applicant has not thought through the relevant issues (or even worse, the legal implications) at all. Of course, the opposite may be true. After a few forms, it is easy to get 'good' at complying with institutional procedures. This raises the possibility that researchers might get excellent at filling in ethics forms but not be very ethical in their practices. In the absence of compliance procedures, this is for the most part a matter for their own consciences.

Quick question

After approval, many ethics forms are never looked at again. Do you think there should be procedures to check if you conducted the study ethically (e.g. ethical audits?) What would be the disadvantages?

SUMMARY

The overall aim of making a written ethics application or completing a project on ethics is to display, in writing, 'ethical competence'. This can be accomplished in seven basic steps:

1. Identify the institutional requirements, correct forms and timeline for submission.
2. Write a rough draft for each section.
3. Check against the key mistakes in this chapter and make any necessary changes.
4. Get another student, colleague, supervisor or ethics officer to review the final version.
5. Submit the correct forms by the deadline to the correct person.
6. Make any amendments as soon as they are received.
7. File the application, the certificate and any other ethics documents securely.

Ethical Dilemma 5: A rejected ethics application

Manda has got an opportunity to study a group of veterans from the Vietnam War through her uncle who is part of a veterans group. She has written a proposal for the IRB at her institution laying out her research design. She is mindful of the need not to cause distress, so proposes only to interview them about the positive aspects of being in a veterans group and how this extends the camaraderie forged in the war itself. She is astonished when the IRB reject her proposal because of 'poor design' and insufficient understanding of the ethical harms. She is considering making an appeal, but doesn't know anyone else who has done this.

1. Do you think this study is poorly designed, if so, why? Does that make it unethical?
2. What do you think Manda should do to resolve the situation?
3. In what situations should IRBs/committees be challenged? What are some of the reasons this rarely happens?

6 Ethical Dilemmas When Running Projects

From the lifecycle approach to research ethics, thinking about ethical issues doesn't stop once you get the approval certificate. This section examines how research ethics can play out in the course of a project. The issues that arise are not necessarily those predicted in the ethics application, but reflect the embedded nature of a researcher's role, working in a real world with real people. This chapter focuses on several common issues: (1) *Handling participant distress* including handling upset, complaints or withdrawal from the study; (2) *whether to intervene* in cases of social problems, criminal acts or abuse; and (3) *ending the research relationship* at the end of a project. I also argue for agreeing an expanded version of 'confidentiality' with participants to promote ethical discussion and problem-solving.

THE PRACTICE OF EVERYDAY RESEARCH ETHICS

Everyday research ethics is about what happens after ethical approval is given and data collection starts. Inevitably, unexpected ethical issues arise as you conduct your research in practice, which Guillemin and Gillam term 'ethically important moments' (Guillemin & Gillam, 2004). These are not necessarily 'ethical dilemmas' in the classical sense, but are primarily (although not always) small-scale issues that arise from interacting with humans. Guillemin and Gillam's proposal is that researchers should cultivate what they term 'ethical reflexivity'. By this they mean thinking critically about your behaviour as a researcher, your participants as humans with needs, and the context you find yourself in, in an ethically reflexive way. They have also referred to this as 'ethical mindfulness', which means being aware of ethics in everyday practice.

I find it helpful to think about everyday ethics in terms of 'ethically important moments'. However there are two additional points to make. Firstly, 'ethically important moments' need discussion. It is difficult to develop ethical mindfulness by yourself. Even highly experienced researchers who have been in their field for 25 years can come across troubling or sensitive situations which leave them feeling unsure about what is ethical to do or how to proceed. Ethics systems should not leave students or staff alone with their ethical issues. Many funded projects, particularly those with significant ethical issues from the outset (e.g. research into abuse or criminal behaviour or terrorism), require a 'chain of command' so that if an ethical issue arises, there is a clear pathway of people to consult and make decisions (e.g. there may be a project ethics advisory board). If you are a student or researcher working on your own, then the most obvious place to start with any ethical discussion is with a supervisor, followed by an ethics officer or representative. The section at the end of this chapter considers how to negotiate confidentiality/the need for discussion with participants.

Secondly, as argued in Chapter 5, ethical mindfulness shouldn't tip over into ethical hyper-sensitivity. As with any profession where you come into contact with the public, ethical awareness is important. However, it is not necessary to over-analyse every interaction for ethical aspects. A healthy regard for ethics, and being able to spot and handle particularly tricky situations, is enough.

Quick question

Have you had any 'ethically important moments'? What were they? Do you wish you had handled them differently?

HANDLING PARTICIPANT DISTRESS, COMPLAINTS OR WITHDRAWAL

Participant distress

Very few researchers conducting qualitative research such as interviews or participant observation will have never seen a

end. One tangible way of displaying respect for the seriousness of some parts of the stories was to offer to 'turn the tape off' if something particularly upsetting was revealed. Although participants rarely wanted this, it somehow acted as a marker of respect for the traumatic nature of the stories, which were above and beyond the 'usual'. No complaints were made and nobody withdrew from the study.

Withdrawing from a study

Your consent form or procedure states that participants should be able to withdraw from the study, without giving a reason. Even if this makes life difficult for you as the researcher, you must honour this by letting people withdraw without making them feel bad or questioning their decision. In most large-scale projects I've worked on, one or two people have withdrawn. They might spontaneously give a reason, such as a death in the family, or just decide now is not the right time to stay in a study. You should not question them on this if they don't offer a reason, but simply take their details and withdraw them politely. It is fine to ask if they want all their data deleted or whether you can use the data to that time point. Often people withdraw from a study because they don't want to be involved in the future, but are fine with you using previously collected data. One option is to offer the right to withdraw up to a specified time point (e.g. the start of analysis) so that the researcher does not spend further time on unusable material. It also raises the question of whether individuals or organizations should have the right to 'veto' or pre-screen a publication if they feel maligned or unhappy with the interpretation of data collected with consent. Ethically this brings into conflict the principles of 'informed consent' and 'academic freedom'.

SHOULD YOU INTERVENE?

Intervening to help participants

Whether you are confronted with this particular 'ethical moment' will depend a lot on the type of project. If it is one which focuses on a problem for which intervention may be appropriate, then building in help may need to be an integral part of the design. For example, if you were interviewing teenagers with eating disorders, then preparing for requests for help, or offering sources of help (e.g. helpline numbers or access to counselling) is sensible.

Issues around intervention may also be pronounced if you are forming long-term relationships with your participants, for example, in an ethnographic study. Here, you have a dual role: as a researcher but also as a member of that community. Researchers may not have any legal or professional 'obligation' to intervene (or they may, see below). However, our roles as humans who care for others may lead us to feel the need to do things to help. Again, such intervention can fit within an 'ethics of care' approach, which prioritizes relationships and trust. On the other hand, researchers have limited roles and are not therapists, counsellors or health professionals. Helping the person seek help rather than offer it yourself is therefore more appropriate.

There are times when intervention may be more serious, such as if a participant is suffering sexual, physical or another type of abuse (e.g. neglect), or describes perpetrating/it occurring to others. The legal obligation to disclose this varies from country to country, and depends on the role. For example, in the UK, social workers, teachers and other health professionals have a duty to disclose abuse to the authorities as part of their professional codes and could face disciplinary proceedings/legal action if they did not. Researchers, on the other hand, have no such legal 'duty of care' even if there is a moral one. If you think someone is suffering from or perpetrating abuse, then immediately seek advice from higher up the ethical chain of command. I would personally seek advice (and have given advice myself) from an experienced ethics officer/Chair of an IRB/Advisory Board. As the case study in Chapter 1 indicated, some behaviour (e.g. in areas like caring for elders or children) falls into a 'grey' area between 'undesirable' and 'abusive', and trying to decide what colour it is is something no researcher should do alone. Furthermore, if confidentiality has been promised to participants, then most researchers would want to discuss the breaking of this confidentiality with the participant directly, before going ahead with a disclosure that could have many ramifications.

Seeking knowledgeable others to discuss the case in confidence has to be the starting point.

Example: Intervention

Moments concerning intervention can come up unexpectedly. In my small-scale study of men and health/illness, one participant talked for a while about hangovers and sports injuries, when he paused, and said 'I've had a hard lump on my testicles for two years but have never told anyone'. I did not feel it was appropriate to just carry on in a dispassionate way. Rightly or wrongly, I intervened, switched off the tape, and talked at length to the participant about seeing a doctor. I am not a health professional, so had no knowledge of if this was the right thing to do, but I did what I would do for a friend in this situation, which is advise them to seek medical advice. This could be positioned within an 'ethics of care', which prioritizes an emotional 'duty to care' relationship (Gilligan, 1982), although I did not consciously think of this at the time.

Reporting threats or criminal acts

Over the years, going into the houses of many people, I have witnessed, or heard discussion of, what I consider to be minor crimes, such as smoking cannabis/other drug use, claiming benefits when out of work, or people living together but claiming to be single, again to get governmental support. I had never thought much of this until I attended a research seminar on ethics. One of the topics was whether the researcher had a 'duty' to report such crimes. To my astonishment, one of the course leaders argued quite strongly that we should all report these as crimes in an active way. I felt quite strongly the opposite, that having promised confidentiality and anonymity to our participants, it should only be broken in the most serious of cases. I also could not see how research with marginalized groups or criminals could occur if essentially researchers operated as pseudo-policemen; who would ever participate and expose themselves to the risk of being reported? At a social level, there is a strong rationale for studying why people engage in illegal behaviours such as violence, criminal acts or use illegal drugs, even acts of terrorism. These topics can prove problematic for IRBs/ ethics committees (e.g. Adler & Adler, 2002) as institutional and legal requirements not to be complicit in illegal activities can conflict with the need to preserve anonymity and confidentiality.

If your project carries an inherent risk of uncovering and documenting illegal activities, then this needs to be dealt with upfront during the design/ethical approval stage. Options include in the US obtaining a 'waiver', which protects participants by giving them confidentiality (see Hot Topic Chapter 8), collecting no identifiable data or stating the need for potential disclosure upfront to participants before beginning any research, so they can choose how much or little to disclose. If your project is not focused on illegal activities, but you encounter them as part of everyday research (as is fairly inevitable in the forms I describe at the beginning), then, again, discussion with a supervisor/ethics officer for some informal advice is a good starting point. Where it ends up will depend very much on the nature of the criminal act and the consequences of not disclosing.

ENDING THE RESEARCH RELATIONSHIP

In some types of research, ending the research relationship is not particularly problematic. If you invite participants to take part in an experiment, complete a survey or be interviewed as a one-off, then the research experience has a natural arc; the idea of the study is presented, the data is collected and the study ends by thanking them for participating. Clarity about what will happen during the research process makes this even more straightforward; I usually spend some time outlining this before enrolling participants.

As with intervening during data collection, it may also be appropriate to direct participants to further information or sources of help at the end of research. For example, Brabeck and Brabeck (2009) conducting a qualitative research study about intimate partner abuse with Mexican women provided information about domestic abuse legislation and solid advice about accessing services. Ending the research relationship well in this sense is not just about interpersonal ethics, but about social justice.

However, in other types of research, such as longer-term or ethnographic research, the ending may be less clear and easily negotiated. There may be multiple reasons for this. One may be that the research population may be vulnerable in some sense, and so misunderstandings about the nature of the researcher–researched relationship may occur. I discuss this in relation to people with learning disability in Chapter 10 where the increased interest due to research can be perceived as friendship (Thompson, 2002). One researcher I heard of used to wear a badge saying 'I'm a researcher' on it when working with a vulnerable population, so their dual identity as carer/researcher was made visible. Secondly, it may simply be due to the length of time spent with participants which allows greater intimacy and relationships to be built. This is particularly the case with ethnographic research in which being embedded in the culture under observation is an integral part of the method. Furthermore, there may not be a distinct end to research; the researcher may go in and out of the research arena over a number of years. One way to provide closure is to work together on or show participants analysis and publication material. This focuses everyone on the end of the research lifecycle in a natural way. This may not be an easy process, especially if brings to the fore that the researcher is still, whatever friendships may have been forged, a researcher who has collected valuable information for their own goals, even if these were made clear and aligned with goals in the community. Other relationships may endure after the end of 'official' data collection.

Example: A good ending

Although conducting one-off interviews means that the 'ending' of the research encounter is obvious, this does not always mean it is easy, particularly if sensitive or disturbing material has been revealed within it, even if this experience appears cathartic to the participant. In my small-scale study on men and illness/health, there was a need to reassure participants who had disclosed particularly sensitive information that their stories are 'held safely', both in emotional and practical terms. This involved reassuring participants about anonymity, confidentiality and good data protection, as well as thanking them genuinely for what they shared.

CONFIDENTIALITY AND ETHICAL DISCUSSION

When ethical 'moments' arise in your own everyday research, it can be very helpful to talk with others, colleagues, a supervisor or an ethics officer. However, does this break the principle of confidentiality for the participant? The obvious answer is that it depends how confidentiality was framed for the participant in the consent process. It can be helpful to offer confidentiality within the research team, rather than with one individual. For a student, the research team might be themselves and a supervisor. For a postgraduate or researcher, this might be a wider team, such as other research assistants or colleagues working specifically on that particular project, including the transcriber. I do not see this as a breach of confidentiality, any more than I would consider it unethical for a counsellor to discuss a difficult case with their lead therapist, or a doctor to share notes within a doctors' surgery (both of which happen). However, if confidentiality has been offered on a completely individual basis (between one participant and one researcher alone), then ethical discussion can only take place if you either anonymize the discussion completely (which can lead to crucial contextual details being missed out) or to break confidentiality in serious cases.

Everyday ethics flourishes where people can discuss cases and consider different points of view; it is (in my view) not necessarily ethical, or in the participants' best interests to constrain such discussion with a very heavy interpretation of 'confidentiality'.

SUMMARY

Ethically tricky moments do arise in most research projects. There is no 'right' answer to dealing with them, as each one will concern very different participants in distinct scenarios. The key to handling them is to have developed a good ethical sense and know the 'chain of command' (or who to seek advice from) if they go beyond your own expertise and to gain alternative perspectives.

This second part of the book has covered research ethics from a lifecycle perspective, in which ethics is embedded in the practices of everyday research. Within this lifecycle, gaining ethical approval is the formalized part of demonstrating ethical competence and meeting institutional requirements. Dealing with ethical issues at the design stage and whilst running a project are equally important informal settings in which research ethics are practiced. The next part of this book focuses on key 'Hot Topics' within research ethics. These offer greater detail on classic topics (e.g. informed consent, assessment of possible harm) as well as newer ones (e.g. Internet research, researcher safety), which can be drawn on both when writing ethics proposals and as a basis for wider ethical discussion.

CASE STUDY: WHEN YOUR PARTICIPANT TAKES A DEEP BREATH...

Having conducted several studies on health and illness using narrative approaches which aim to elicit people's stories, I am now alert for what I term 'the deep breath moment'. This is when the interviewee pauses, or shifts a bit, perhaps looks away, and takes a deep breath, before telling you something which to them is highly significant in terms of their life story. For example, in the study of men's perceptions of health and illness, my very first question in the interview schedule was 'what comes into your mind when I say the word 'health'?' In a couple of instances, participants paused, took a deep breath and then went on to tell about very traumatic events, such as the death of a loved one in highly distressing or unexpected circumstances. Initially I was taken aback. I had imagined having a discussion about health in general as a concept, but literally moments into the interview, we were dealing death and trauma. Similar 'deep breath' moments have included covering topics such as miscarriages, death of children, past sexual abuse, fatal accidents, family secrets and so on. When a deep breath moment occurs, it would feel disrespectful to just continue with the interview schedule in a dispassionate way. I sometimes offer to turn the tape off, sometimes not; either way I just sit and listen. For participants, this seems a cathartic experience, although there is always the worry that you have stirred up old emotions. Not everyone has such tales, or wants to share them with a researcher. If they do arise, it is a question of sensitively negotiating the sharing of human experience and emotion for which there simply isn't a protocol for 'getting it right'.

Ethical Dilemma 6: Should you intervene?

There are two different case studies here. Read both and answer the questions given after them.

Case Study 1

John is working as a research assistant on a project interviewing teenage boys about their attitude towards school, education and attending college. He is interviewing them in pairs (dyadic interviews). The sample is from diverse schools in different neighbourhoods. In one of the interviews, the two boys talk about relations with a neighbouring school and reveal that they have planned to 'fight' a group of other boys from this school in a couple of days time, to settle a score over a perceived disrespect, although they quickly stop talking about it. John will not be talking to them again till the following week. He is not sure what to do next, if anything, although he has thought about mentioning it to a teacher. His imagination is now running riot and he is worried in case one of the boys gets stabbed and he didn't say anything.

Case Study 2

Bronwyn was working as a researcher interviewing women living in hostels as part of a government-funded project on how families cope in temporary accommodation. One of her interviewees is a young woman with two children. Whenever she has visited, the husband has not been present. During one of the interviews, this woman says 'it is better he is not here, otherwise things go wrong'. When Bronwyn probes further, the woman reveals that he has beaten her up two weeks ago. She begs Bronwyn not to tell anyone, not even her colleagues, as otherwise 'he

---

might find out'. She appears terrified. Bronwyn has another interview in a month with this woman and is very worried about what might happen in the meantime.

1. What are the implications in each case if the researcher broke confidentiality and told someone in 'authority'?
2. What does an 'ethic of care' which prioritizes interpersonal relation-ships and helping the less powerful (see also Chapter 2) add to these dilemmas over intervention?
3. For each case, imagine that the researcher has asked you what to do: what would you advise them?

Part III
Ethical 'Hot Topics'

7 Informed Consent

This 'Hot Topics' chapter aims to offer two things. Firstly, it outlines the key issues about informed consent, looking at critical perspectives as well as standard practice. Secondly, it gives practical advice on how to create your own consent forms and procedures to meet IRB/ethics committee requirements and, more importantly, produce ethically acquired data.

Specific guidance on consent with (a) vulnerable groups and (b) children is found in other Hot Topics. If you are researching with these groups, do read those additional sections carefully as consent in those contexts has legal as well as moral aspects.

WHAT IS INFORMED CONSENT?

Informed consent is probably the cornerstone of ethical practice in Western research (Charbonneau, 1984, cited in van den Hoonaard, 2002, p. 9). As discussed in Chapter 2, it is an application of the principle of 'respect for persons' outlined in the Belmont Code. There are three aspects of informed consent: information, comprehension and voluntariness. The aim of informed consent is to allow the participant or group to make an 'autonomous' decision (i.e. an independent one), with enough relevant information, enough understanding (i.e. the capacity to consent) and no pressure to participate. Impaired capacity or inability to consent refers to impairment in one of these areas. This might be a problem with retaining or processing information, comprehending the choice to participate, or a compromise in the voluntariness of participation. It can occur through certain conditions (e.g. stroke, physical impairment, Alzheimer's), or within groups (e.g. those with learning disabilities). For more on consent when there is impaired capacity, see Hot Topic 'Vulnerable

Groups' (Chapter 10). Children and other vulnerable groups may also require more creative and tailored consent procedures (Thompson, 2002).

Ensuring 'informed consent' or rather 'informed and voluntary participation' is accepted as a pre-requisite by most social researchers (Burgess, 2007). However, there is considerable controversy on how to deliver it (Corrigan, 2003; Murphy & Dingwall, 2007). Debates have centred on whether medical models of written consent are appropriate in social science, how to ensure consent in long-term projects and whether covert research without consent is ever justified (Boulton & Parker, 2007; Burgess, 2007; Miller & Boulton, 2007; Wiles, Heath, Crow, & Charles, 2005).

WHAT SHOULD GO IN A CONSENT FORM?

Informed consent is, for the most part, delivered through asking participants to sign a written consent form. There are certain basic parameters to creating this form. In some countries, these are specified, such as in the US by federal regulations (e.g. see Sieber, 2000, p. 33). Sample consent forms may be provided for you to use. These can then be adapted to your target population. The key task is to make the form understandable to ordinary people who do not have specialist scientific knowledge. I was always advised to write a consent form for adults at a level that the average 11-year-old (5th/ 6th grader) could read. Consent forms also need to be in the appropriate language for participants (so more than one version may need to be produced). For example, for those with learning disabilities, materials in Easy Read (accessible to those with lower literacy levels) may be appropriate.

Key points to include (a brief couple of lines on each):

1. Identify who you are personally and from which institution.
2. Explain who funds the study.
3. Say what your study is about. This may be where, if deception is necessary, you do not put full details of the purpose of the study, and these can be included in the 'debrief' at the end.

4. Describe what will happen to the participant and how long it will take.
5. Describe any potential risks/harms. If the risks are not minimal, then explain if there are any treatments/services offered to mitigate these (e.g. help lines, counselling, to contact GP).
6. Describe any benefits of participating.
7. Outline that confidentiality and anonymity will be offered in the study and explain what that means. If there are limits on confidentiality/anonymity, or it is not possible, explain this clearly.
8. Explain participants have a right to withdraw at any time during the study without giving a reason.
9. Explain participants do not have to take part and that this does not affect their care/access to services or other aspect of their usual involvement in any way.
10. Give the contact details of the researcher, as well as an 'independent' person who can be contacted if there are any problems (e.g. for a student, the supervisor; for a researcher, the head of department, ethics officer or other figure in authority).
11. Invite them to participate by signing and dating a copy of the form along with the researcher, keeping one copy each.

Some researchers, including myself, prefer to create a separate information sheet and consent form, with the information sheet containing the bulk of these details. The consent form can then be in the form of tick boxes to sentences such as *I consent to take part in the study X* and *I understand my data will be kept confidential and anonymous within the research team*.

A sample consent form and information sheet is included at the end of Chapter 12. Many institutions/IRBs also provide online samples; if so, I would use that one rather than mine to fulfil their requirements.

ORAL CONSENT

Using written consent forms has become a normative practice within much social science research (Van den Hoonaard, 2002). However, many researchers have argued that asking participants to sign on the dotted line is not only impractical in some settings, but unethical (e.g. Coomber, 2002). There are a variety of reasons given for not wanting to use a written consent in all studies:

1. People in disadvantaged groups or on the margins of society may associate signatures/forms with 'authority' and not wish to participate.
2. It can establish a culture of 'mistrust' between researcher and researched by making the agreement seem 'legal' and not a matter of mutual understanding.
3. In some cultures, it is not clear who needs to sign, as consent may be more collectively understood (e.g. senior gatekeepers may consent for the group).
4. Carrying signed consent form may compromise the safety of the researcher or the researched in dangerous or legally compromising situations (e.g. for criminals).
5. Participants may be illiterate or have a limited ability to understand written material.
6. Signed consent identifies people. If you are doing a survey on illegal drug use, it may be better not to collect identifying details, taking the returning of a questionnaire as a sign of consent (behavioural consent) (see Common Rule Section 46.117 (c)).

There can also be cultural issues around written consent. Informed consent of the individual may be the cornerstone of all Western ethical codes but does not necessarily 'make sense' in non-Western contexts. In much of the Middle East, for example, a researcher arriving with armfuls of information sheets and asking for signatures can be perceived as strange at best, and distrustful at worst:

> ...the very idea of written information sheets and especially consent sheets is normally a no-no, as it tends to frighten people away and certainly undermines the very most essential element necessary for success: the establishment of personal trust. It creates 'distance'. At best, it would be seen as highly peculiar by interviewees or 'human sources' (formal or informal) in the region.
>
> (Nonneman, personal communication, 13 January 2011)

Cultural differences therefore need to be taken into account when designing consent procedures. One strategy that has worked well with many Arab and Middle Eastern students researching in their home countries has been to carry an official letter from the university, stating who they are and what they are doing. This is then used alongside oral consent. The Common Rule allows IRBs to authorize oral informed consent under certain circumstances, such as if the research is minimal risk and it would be culturally inappropriate to use written consent (Section 46.117c).

In the vast majority of cases, seeking written consent is ethically unproblematic. It has been criticized for imposing a legalistic and contract-type relationship between researcher and participant (e.g. Dingwall, 2006). However it may be, this fits well with our already bureaucratic culture; many participants find the paperwork which confirms 'we are who we say we are' to be reassuring. An ethical researcher needs to be flexible though; more than once I have interviewed someone who is semi-literate or completely illiterate (which they may not want to tell you directly). In these instances, it would be incredibly insensitive to insist they complete all forms. Tape-recording consent is a more than adequate alternative. However, there is a strong reason not to rely solely on oral consent; people find it difficult to retain spoken information, even more so if they are stressed or emotional about a topic (e.g. Kessels, 2003). Providing written documents provides valuable and lasting information, so that when they go away, they have an answer to the question *who was that lady and what did I agree to again?'* Using oral consent should therefore be used only where written materials are in some way compromising to the project, and justified clearly in ethics applications. The Common Rule Section 46.116 (d) allows IRBs to waiver informed consent or approve alternatives if the research is no more than minimal risk, there is no harm to participants from the changes, the research can't be carried out without the changes and that additional information will be provided if appropriate after participation. The AAA's Statement on Ethnography and IRB's on oral consent is also useful (American Anthropological Association, 2004).

Key questions to consider when using oral consent

1. Why is the use of oral consent justified? Will any written materials be provided?

2. What will you say? Including bullet points or a short sample text shows you have thought through what to say in the field.
3. How will participants be able to contact you once you have left the field? (e.g. to withdraw, review their involvement, see the results of the study. Some researchers leave a card with contact details/sheet in the local language, for example, or contact details through gatekeepers and organizations on the ground).

Sample oral consent text (needs to be briefer than written consent so people can retain it):

My name is Hannah Farrimond, I'm a researcher from X university, and I'm doing some research into what people think about Type 2 diabetes in this country. I'm going to tell you a bit about the study and then ask you if you'd be happy to take part, is that ok? I'm funded by an international organization X, you know, the people who sponsor the health-care clinic in the next town. The purpose of doing this project is to try to understand how people think about Type 2 diabetes. If you take part, I will come and interview you about your experiences with diabetes. The aim is to understand how we can talk about diabetes in a way that people understand. If you agree, I'll record your interview on my digital recorder. I won't use your name and I won't tell anyone else about what you say to me, except others in my research team. You could also leave the study at any time without giving a reason by contacting Y (here's her card). Would you like to take part? Do you have any questions?

A final note, I personally use both oral and written consent together: providing written information to get over the details and a bit of discussion to clarify any misunderstandings. Written and oral consent need not be considered polar opposites but complementary ways of ensuring robust consent.

COMMUNITY/LEVELS OF CONSENT

Negotiating consent

Informed consent is usually thought of as an individual process. However, there are research situations where other levels of consent may need to be sought. People who allow/offer access to participants or a research field are known as 'gatekeepers'. If you planned to do a small-scale research project about a local business, for example, it would not be ethical (or socially acceptable) to directly contact workers in the business to arrange interviews on site without getting permission from the overall boss. Similarly, schools and child-care settings, medical care/health care services, religious groups, companies and community groups, to name just a few, have hierarchical organizational structures which needs to be addressed by consent procedures. In these settings, consent often becomes complex and takes place at multiple layers, which is why I call it a 'web of consent' (see the Case Study).

In a hierarchical group, institution or organization, it is usual to ask permission to research from the gatekeepers or key authority before approaching other participants. This can be negotiated in person and confirmed in writing. Information sheets, consent forms and a copy of the protocol should be provided. Harms and benefits need to be expressed at the appropriate level, specifying what these are for the overall organization, company or community as well as for individuals. Anonymity and confidentiality need to be carefully negotiated. This is because although anonymity and confidentiality can be assured for individuals, it may not be possible, or even desirable, to anonymize the name of the community, institution or company (see Hot Topic Chapter 8). Gatekeepers will usually discuss possible participation with other key people in their group or organization before taking a decision.

Technically, many ethical guidelines state that observation in a public space does not need consent. However, there are places in which the public and private are conflated (e.g. a church or religious space, a public library). In these, it is sensible to ask gatekeepers for permission to observe, particularly with topics that may be sensitive. The AAA also points out that community authorities may also need to approve the research, for example, in developing world research, so as not to put participants at risk of community sanction (American Anthropological Association, 2004). They also state that spouse or male-household head 'may be the culturally or legally appropriate agent to provide consent', which raises the ethical dilemma presented in Chapter 2 concerning how to handle consent where women's autonomy is culturally low.

Ensuring voluntariness in groups

One ethical difficulty that can arise where gatekeepers have already given permission is that individuals may then find it difficult to refuse (i.e. they are unintentionally caught in the 'web of consent', if you like). For example, doing research with law enforcement or the military typically involves extensive negotiation with key gatekeepers to get agreement to participate and access to the field. Once this is given, officers or staff may be told to participate rather than invited. One way to tackle this is to be very transparent with gatekeepers that individual consent will still be sought. Equally, you should reiterate to participants at the point of data collection that their participation should be entirely voluntary.

Issues over voluntariness are often not a matter of coercion, more a subtle pressure to participate. Gatekeeper/researchers sometimes find it difficult to understand that others may not want to do so. Our committee had a rash of applications from very enthusiastic vicars (pastors) who were all sure that their congregation or group would love to participate in their study, but who clearly hadn't considered the issue of how some of them might gracefully withdraw without offending their spiritual leader. Furthermore, gatekeepers may have their own agendas for wanting to see research conducted, which may conflict with the needs of the study population. For example, professionals in palliative care have raised questions about whether dying patients always benefit from research practices, for example, such as interviews which may tax them physically and mentally (Lawton, 2001).

OBSERVING PUBLIC BEHAVIOUR AND CONSENT

Within most social science codes, observing people in public places is not considered a matter for seeking 'informed consent'. This is because people do not expect to be private in a public place, and being observed by others is a reasonable thing to occur (e.g. we are observed by other people, CCTV). There is also a methodological issue. One of the key reasons to do ethnographic research is to get as real a picture as possible, disturbing the field as little as possible

(Hammersley & Atkinson, 1995). Continuously informing people you are a researcher, and seeking their consent, could be highly intrusive and disturbing.

However, this does not mean that the requirement for informed consent should be abandoned in all ethnographic or observational studies. If it is a partially closed area (e.g. a shop, conference, GP's surgery) where the public can enter, it is best practice to seek the consent of key gatekeepers (e.g. shop manager, religious leader, head of a clinic and so on) and discuss how they want consent to operate after that. Often an 'opt-out' model is used, so your presence as a researcher could be shared by leaflets, emailing all staff or during a meeting. Ideally you can then give a brief explanation of your project, and ask that if anyone does not want to participate that they inform you. This allows you to conduct participant observation freely in that field without compromising consent. If more in-depth data (e.g. interviews) are conducted, individual consent can be sought for these in the usual manner. How often and in what ways consent should be negotiated in long-term ethnographic research in which the researcher is embedded in the community continues to be a matter for debate (Brewer, 2000).

DEBRIEFING

Debriefing is a term used in psychological and behavioural research. It means giving information about the study after the data collection has been completed. This could be verbal feedback such as 'what we were measuring here was your heart-rate in response to the pictures'. Often written debriefing is required where deception has been used. This should cover the purpose of the task, how and why participants were deceived and give an opportunity to ask questions. As such, it represents an opportunity for 'closure' for the participant who goes away fully informed. Debriefing can also involve correcting minor harms that might have occurred within the data collection. For example, if the experiment involved inducing a bad mood, then usually debriefing would include doing an additional task to restore the previous mood. If the harm of being debriefed outweighs the benefit (e.g. revealing that people were being tested to see if they were prejudiced), there is an argument for not doing it. If you are doing a psychological or behavioural experiment or study, you should include details of how you will debrief in your ethics protocol.

Quick question

What are the advantages or disadvantages of seeking consent throughout the lifecycle of a research project? At what time points should consent be sought?

CONSENT-AS-PROCESS

There has been a move towards considering consent procedures in research as a process, rather than as a one-off event defined by a signature on a form (Cutliffe & Ramcharan, 2002; Ramcharan & Cutliffe, 2001). The rationale for a consent-as-process approach is strongest within ethnographic research. It is argued that too little of the research process is specified in advance to ask participants to consent only once at the start. Although typically ethnographers set out with a research site or set of questions in advance, much of the research process unfolds in situ. Furthermore, the analysis and uses these might have (e.g. on contentious or sensitive issues) cannot be predicted before data is collected. It therefore makes sense to seek consent throughout the process in a participatory fashion. The need for consent across time is not exclusive to ethnographic studies, however. For example, if a parent consents for a newborn to take part in a longitudinal cohort study, then consent may also be re-sought from the child and parent at secondary age and from the child alone at the age of majority. Consent may also be sought repeatedly for tests or samples.

Another situation in which repeated consent is indicated is where there is fluctuating capacity to consent. Guidelines suggest that in this instance (e.g. with dementia, Alzhemier's, stroke, terminal illness), consent may need to be sought at every data collection time point. For example, if a researcher visits someone with early-stage dementia over several months, they may need to seek consent at the start of each visit and watch for signs/direct expression of dissent/ withdrawal of participation. Wider issues of overall withdrawal should be discussed with the carer/proxy as well as the participant (see Hot Topic 'Vulnerable Groups and Sensitive Topics' for a further discussion of this (Chapter 10)).

There are several issues with consent-as-process. One of these is simply that it may be very annoying if someone keeps asking you if you still want to participate. In ethnographic studies, it may be intrusive in the sense indicated by Hammersley and Atkinson; it may damage the 'reality' of the situation. Secondly, repeatedly asking for consent raises the probable rate of refusal, although it could be argued that this is an ethical reason to keep asking, not ask less. Thirdly, it is not clear how repeated consent should be conducted and documented – should it be in a series of signatures, or just oral consent? Despite these issues, consent-as-process make sense within certain research contexts, such as long-term research, and may happen more automatically if a participatory approach is used (e.g. as participants express their consent by being involved at numerous time points).

DECEPTION AND COVERT RESEARCH

In a recent review of covert research, Spicker (2011) makes a distinction between 'deception', in which the participants are deceived as to the purpose of the study, and 'covert research', in which the research participants do not know they are taking part. This is a useful distinction, because although both deception and covert research both challenge the principle of informed consent, they require a different set of practical considerations.

Deception

Deception was, and still is, a relatively common practice in experimental and behavioural traditions such as psychology (Kimmel, 1996). Deception can take place in several ways. The participant may not be informed of the purpose of the study, may be misinformed before or during the study, or otherwise deceived (e.g. the study may involve researchers pretending to be participants to create an experimental scenario). The justification for such deception is that if participants were fully informed, it might either prime them to change their behaviour, or prevent the behaviour being studied at all. It is thus conceptualized as a way of increasing validity.

Example (without deception): You are asked to participate in an experiment about group behaviour towards a stigmatized condition (e.g. a visible facial disfigurement). You are told the purpose from the start in the consent form. In the experiment, you modify your behaviour (e.g. not showing your natural reactions) so as not to seem stigmatizing.

Example (with deception): You are asked to participate in an experiment about group behaviour. You are not told the purpose from the start of the study. You act as you normally would within the experiment. You are told afterwards (debriefing) that the study was investigating if people stigmatize those with facial disfigurements.

Many famous studies in psychology involve deception. One example is the bystander apathy set of experiments (Darley & Latane, 1968; Latane & Darley, 1969). Following the murder of a young woman who many people ignored when she cried for help, Darley and Latane experimentally investigated the conditions in which people did or did not respond in emergencies. Participants were confronted with a series of unexpected events, such as the experiment room filling with smoke or another participant having an epileptic fit (this was really a pre-recorded tape of a researcher pretending to need medical help). It is arguable that had they told their participants in advance what they were studying, participants would not have responded authentically.

There has been a backlash against deceptive practices in research. Codes such as the British Psychological Society make it clear that participants should not be misled or deceived 'without extremely strong scientific or medical justification' (British Psychological Society, 2009, p. 10). The key issue is that deception violates informed consent, as the participant is not informed of the true purpose of the study, so is choosing to participate on false knowledge.

Participants may feel a bit stupid or duped, or even that they would not have participated had they known, although they still have the option to withdraw once the deception is revealed. Other objections to deception/covert research centre on the effect on the research relationship. It could lead to a breakdown of trust in individual researchers, and in research as a social enterprise ('polluting the research environment'), as well as habituating the researcher to deception as a normal practice (Homan, 1991, 1992).

If you are intending to mislead or deceive participants, then this will need to be addressed explicitly in the ethics application. This would include explaining (a) why the procedure is justified, at a scientific level and why alternatives are not possible; (b) that there is a well-thought out debriefing procedure (see above section on 'debriefing') and (c) how this deception and debrief is likely to be received within the community it is intended for, for example, by conducting a pilot debrief.

Questions if you are intending to use deception

- Is the use of deception strongly justified? Are there any alternatives?
- Is any harm likely to occur as a result of the deception? (e.g. distress at being deceived)
- How will you debrief the participants?

One small note: some IRBs/ethics committees insist on the whole academic study title being used on the consent forms so that it is clear this is a consent form matching a recognized and certified study. However, sometimes study titles, used to explain the purpose to other academics or funders, are overly priming for participants. Using the example above, a study entitled 'What drives the stigmatization of the facially disfigured?' is going to prime any participant that it is their reaction to facial disfigurement that is being measured. There is a good argument for modifying study titles to a generic one ('Study on how people respond to different group conditions') so as not to prime participants; there is no reason not to inform them afterwards of the correct title in any debrief.

Covert research

Covert research involves studying participants who are unaware that they are being studied. In the past, covert research often involved participant observation methods in ethnographic research, in which the researcher observed the community 'from the inside' without necessarily mentioning their status as a researcher. Famous covert studies include Laud Humphries' Tearoom Trade (Humphries, 1970) in which he covertly observed male-to-male sexual activities (cottaging) in public toilets and followed participants home and interviewed them without telling them the purpose of his study, thereby revealing the homosexual sex lives of some heterosexual men. The extent to which the covert aspect of this study made it unethical or unjustifiable is still debated (Lenza, 2004).

The main ethical issue with covert research is that 'it violates the principle of informed consent and may invade the privacy of those being studied' (BSA Statement of Ethical Practice). The British Sociological Association also point out that 'covert researchers might need to take account the emerging legal frameworks surrounding the right to privacy' (p. 5). In other words, although there have been many debates about covert research over the last few decades, norms relating to privacy in people's private lives both within and out of research have changed, as has the legal framework around it (e.g. Article 8 of the Human Rights Act 1988 makes provision for a private and family life). This may mean that covert research is less acceptable and less protected than in the past.

So why would researchers choose to override informed consent and conduct covert research? There are several potential reasons:

1. To get research data on everyday practices through observation and other non-obtrusive research methods.

   Example: A researcher wants to understand the constructions of masculinity within football teams, so conducts an auto-ethnography in which they describe their own experiences of belonging to a team for the past 10 years.

2. To get research data on hidden/difficult to access groups, or groups who may refuse to participate, but constitute an important part of social life to study.

   Example: A researcher wants to study Far Right political organizations. They decide to join one, but not reveal their identity to protect themselves and to learn more; identification would lead to the project being abandoned.

3. To get research data on behaviour in institutions or organizations which would otherwise not be uncovered (e.g. unfair or discriminatory practices).

   Example: A governmental/state department claims to treat immigrants in one way, but anecdotal data suggests otherwise. A researcher decides to do a systematic piece of ethnography from the inside the department without telling her bosses.

Some researchers have argued that covert research is intrinsically unethical and constitutes a form of 'spying' on others (Bulmer, 1982). This position asserts that everyone has human rights, including the right to live according to their (legal) life choices, which may or may not include being in someone else's research study. Those who argue for a more nuanced understanding of the potential advantages of covert research point out that many 'overt' (i.e. seeking consent openly) studies nevertheless contain covert practices (Calvey, 2008). These might include not being able to consent everyone in a setting, not reminding people frequently that you are a researcher or appearing less knowledgeable to gain information. Furthermore, they argue, some subjects, or groups, may simply go unstudied by ethnographers if covert research is not allowed (Herrera, 1999; Spicker, 2011).

Covert research has been denormalized to a large extent, so covert studies are likely to come under considerable scrutiny by ethics committees. If you are thinking of conducting, say participant observation with a covert aspect, you should (a) read the literature and disciplinary codes on covert research to have a comprehensive understanding of its merits/demerits and (b) offer a strong justification for covert research for your own particular research question.

Questions if you are intending to use covert methods

- Is the use of covert design strongly justified? Are there any alternatives?
- Is any harm likely to occur as a result of the covert design?
- How will you mitigate these harms? (e.g. give those under study the 'right to reply')

SUMMARY

This section has aimed to give practical advice on how to structure consent forms and procedures, as well as a flavour of the critical thinking around informed consent within social research. The key point is that 'informed consent' is not a static thing, deliverable in only one way, such as through a signed consent form (Miller & Boulton, 2007). Normative standard practices are very useful and appropriate for much social research, which is why I include an example consent form at the end of this book. However, other consent procedures may well be justified.

CASE STUDY: A 'WEB OF CONSENT' IN A STUDY OF LAW ENFORCEMENT

Jesree, a PhD student in her first year, designed a participant observation study within a law enforcement facility to understand the socialization of new recruits in their probationary period. Initial consent was sought at the highest level of law enforcement/police with the Chief of that district. Access to the local facility was negotiated over a six-month period, in which several meetings were held in which the researchers detailed what they wanted to happen in the research and the police responded with their own requirements. Part of these discussions included the consent procedures. It was decided not to observe criminals or members of the public for legal reasons, even though they were present. All inadvertently collected data relating to them (e.g. in conversations with staff, other interactions) was deleted. Participant observation was conducted over a two-month period. All staff were informed by email and during a team meeting that the research was taking place and made it clear who to contact if they did not want to be observed (opt-out). Finally, individual consent was sought from staff members for interviews (opt-in). It was made clear in the consent forms that even though the facility as a whole was participating, individual staff had the right not to participate in interviews. The end result was a 'web of consent', which spread throughout the field site. However, even within this web, not all public members who entered the site were aware they were being observed by a researcher in addition to the usual electronic surveillance.

Ethical Dilemma 7: Permission to observe?

Katrina wanted to observe some religious rituals of a particular religious group. This group often took part in public ceremonies, which Katrina intended to observe as a participant observer in an unobtrusive way. She also wanted to observe prayer meetings and other group activities. Because these were held in a public space in this particular country, she initially assumed that it would be fine to observe without requesting permission. However, on reflection, she thought through what these prayers represented and decided they had both a public (display) function but were also private acts of prayer. She decided to seek the permission of the religious leaders of this group to do observations, viewing them as gatekeepers for the rest of the group. She did not seek informed consent to observe the individuals on a one-to-one basis.

1. What other spaces or situations could be seen as both 'private' and 'public'?
2. Do you think researchers should observe people in prayer? Why or why not?
3. How would issues of informed consent be different if you were a member of the religious group yourself?

---

8 Privacy, Anonymity and Confidentiality

Privacy, anonymity and confidentiality (PAC) are applications of the principle 'respect for persons'. This 'hot topics' chapter briefly defines each of these before looking at practical strategies for implementing them. Common problems with privacy, anonymity and confidentiality are examined, such as how to ensure anonymity in easily identifiable groups or organizations, or when to break confidentiality. Data protection measures are also considered, alongside the issue of how ensuring PAC in an Internet age.

PRIVACY

Privacy is the extent to which you can control how much access others have to your private life, thoughts and feelings. Sieber (1992, p. 49) has some sensible suggestions about how to gauge and think through privacy in your own research, particularly if the topic is a sensitive one. She suggests asking someone who works with the relevant population (e.g. teacher or social worker), talking with other researchers in a similar field and doing pilot work with one or two members of the group to see how they perceive the issue. However, it must be remembered that although some topics will nearly always represent a breach of 'privacy' in a particular community (she cites the example of asking about HIV/AIDS in communities where the topic is taboo), this is not always the case. Different members of the community may perceive the intrusiveness of research differently. Establishing privacy is a sensitive negotiation on the part of the researcher, requiring good emotional literacy to read when people are uncomfortable or distressed by a breach of their privacy.

Issues over privacy also arise in the conducting of research. For example, asking people to participate in front of others for reasons they have not disclosed (e.g. they have a condition or live a certain lifestyle) would breach their privacy. Invitations to participate of this nature should be sent directly to the person. Often it is better to get a 'gatekeeper' such as a GP or consultant to make the initial approach if there are privacy issues surrounding a medical condition. Feeling like your data has been passed on to a university researcher without your knowledge could upset some participants before the project starts. Equally, leaving phone messages such as 'hi, it's the researcher about you taking part in the cancer project' would massively breach privacy on several levels: you don't know if people have disclosed to others that they are participating or that they have cancer. Leaving a neutral name and number is better (although this can provoke suspicion sometimes, I have found).

Arriving to collect your data can also bring up privacy issues. It seems safe to assume that when interviewing family members, you should always interview them separately to ensure privacy. I worked on a project which followed up individuals who had been to their doctors for an intervention. When I arrived at the house to conduct the interviews, I was always made very welcome, but it was clear from the start that most spouses (husbands or wives) thought of this as a joint enterprise, and sat down together to be interviewed about the health issues as a pair. Trying to stick to the protocol, I reiterated quite forcefully that I was just going to ask questions to the individual, and that it would be better to interview them alone. Even then, the spouses wandered in, shouted answers from the kitchen and generally interacted throughout, with the participants' consent ('we haven't any secrets from each other' was a typical response). My idea of privacy was not the same as theirs, and I had to adapt to theirs to make them feel comfortable, whilst also giving the option of individual privacy.

In summary, privacy need to be negotiated with participants in a self-reflexive and sensitive way, as well as delivered through anonymization of the data and ensuring confidentiality.

Quick question

Would you like your own name to be used if you were a research participant? If not, why not? If yes, are there any types of research in which you would rather not be named?

ANONYMITY

Anonymity in the context of research means to disguise, remove or not know the identity of participants. Identifying data includes names, addresses, postcodes/zipcodes and signatures. Other data which gives clues to identity can include job titles, location or a distinctive feature (e.g. having a certain disease or accident). Sometimes it is the combination of information which allows identification. For example, doing research in a local company, X-Corp, you might anonymize names and use job titles 'financial controller at X-Corp', but this may also identify the person easily if there is only one such financial controller. Ensuring anonymity is not just about changing real names, but can involve disguising other identifiable data, such as a place of work, job title or other distinctive detail.

On the other hand, social science data is often rendered meaningful by contexts and detail. If you were doing a study of employer–employee relations in X-Corp, for example, then removing job titles entirely makes the study deficient. Information such as place or job title (to denote position in an organization or socio-economic status) gives situational context and identifies why that participant's data is important. Researchers have to be careful, therefore, that they do not take the anonymization process to the extreme, and render their data less meaningful. This is not particularly ethical if the participant has taken part to no real benefit.

Why is anonymity important?

1. *To ensure the privacy of the participant and the confidentiality of the data.* It allows participants to speak their mind without being identified and perhaps give a window into more private thoughts. It allows participants to participate without others knowing.
2. *To prevent any potential harm of identification.* It allows participants to participate without worrying about the consequences for others, such as family, a partner or friends who may feel upset or betrayed if personal situations are discussed. It also affords them some protection from harms they may not have

anticipated when initially consenting (e.g. if they had expected their names to only appear in a few academic journals and later this research is disseminated widely online).

3. *To conform to data protection requirements.* Data protection requirements do not prevent you from storing personal information, but usually place legal restrictions or require you to register to do so. Research data is usually stored long-term in an anonymized form (see below for more on data protection).

4. *Protect participants and researchers in a legal context from disclosure.* One solution for researchers working in highly sensitive or legally problematic cases (e.g. drug use, criminal activity) is not to collect personal identifiers to prevent requests for disclosure by law enforcement.

Key strategies for anonymization

Each is appropriate for different research designs and scenarios:

1. *Not to collect personally identifiable data.* This is the most secure way of ensuring anonymity. It is appropriate for research where personal identifiers are not necessary, such as survey or online research. In this instance, participants can provide evidence of informed consent by returning the survey or filling in online forms with no names or addresses stored (behavioural consent). As suggested above, not collecting personal identifiers is a good strategy where collecting the data would create a risk of harm (such as need to disclose/risk of arrest) to the participant or the researcher (e.g. studying illegal drug use, criminal activity or when researching in unsafe regimes).

2. *To collect personally identifiable data but remove it from results.* This is the most common practice, probably because other ethical practices, such as asking for written consent, incorporating participant feedback on findings and giving participants a copy of results require the researcher to know the participant's details. There are several ways to decouple identifiable data from findings. One of the easiest is to use a key. To do this, you collect the identifiable data on a separate sheet. You can then assign the rest of the data a participant number or pseudonym (a fake name), remembering to create a key or

system to link the two in case you need to later on. The practice of linking via a participant number is common in both large-scale quantitative studies (e.g. so that participants' results can be linked across years) and smaller qualitative studies in which the researcher often selects a pseudonym when writing up. All of the research data, such as transcripts, document names on computers, digital or tape recordings, documents with results and final outputs should not be stored containing identifying data. Participants are then identified by numbers, pseudonyms or combinations of other information e.g. 'Participant 47, male, shop-floor meat-packer' or 'Cora, mother of two children, one with severe disability'.

3. *To identify the case study, but not the individuals.* In evaluative case studies or ethnographic studies, you may well want to identify the group or organization. This might be because you want to show why this is a useful case study with applicability elsewhere, or because the details of the community are an intrinsic part of the research. It may also be the case that it is not disguisable if it is distinct or the only one of its type (e.g. manufactures a unique product). Yin identifies two levels of anonymity within case studies: that of the entire case (e.g. a whole institution/company/program) and the individuals within the case (Yin, 1994). He argues that anonymity is rarely justified for a whole case, but that anonymity can be offered to individuals through negotiating how they would like to be referred.

4. *Not offer anonymity.* For some individuals, such as those being interviewed in their public capacity, or who are easily identifiable (e.g. CEO of a major corporation, political figure, someone with a public persona), anonymization may not be possible or appropriate. It should be made clear in the consent process that all data collected is going to be cited with the person's real name. Many codes and legal regulations require explicit consent for identified quotes to be used in publication.

Do we always need to anonymize?

Anonymity has become a 'default' practice within research ethics, promoted within ethical codes and underpinned by legislation.

However, the need to preserve anonymity (and privacy/confidentiality) has been questioned. Why?

1. *New challenges to anonymity through the Internet.* The Internet has made it very difficult to anonymize data completely. It is possible to collect non-anonymized online data (e.g. identifiable comments on a site), use it in research in an anonymous form (e.g. changing user names), but then put the 'quote' back into a search engine and arrive at the original non-anonymized data (see Hot Topics on Internet Research).
2. *The practice of anonymization is partly a disciplinary divide.* In oral history, for example, where people are documenting their lives as an oral account of 'what happened', it is common for interviews to be archived using real names.
3. *Some participants are motivated to use their real names.* Participants may be unhappy with their pseudonym or feel their appearance in publications doesn't relate to them (Grinyer, 2002). Naming gives a sense of 'ownership'. Grinyer gives as an example parents whose children died of cancer, where the research seems to have acted as a way of preserving memories, so reading it attached to a pseudonym felt wrong.
4. *There are problems with both using numbers and pseudonyms.* Turning people into a number can seem a bit depersonalizing. Choosing a pseudonym can be equally problematic. Names are distinctive, and tell us something about a person's age and social location. How do you choose an 'equivalent' name and who chooses?
5. *People may be highly recognizable to each other within the confines of a case study or group.* Ethnographic research in a community over a period of years can make it almost impossible to disguise members of the community and the study may not 'make sense' without real identifiable individuals within it. Similarly, research with families means that other members will be able to recognize each other's interviews even if the family as a whole is anonymized.

Despite these arguments, my own view is that there is no good reason to throw out anonymization as the default option just yet. Firstly, anonymization does afford valuable privacy and confidentiality, which encourages research participation. I was interviewed recently on my thoughts on work–life balance for a book which (to my surprise) was serialized in a national newspaper. I didn't want to make a public statement. I was frank because I was offered anonymity. Being anonymous also protected the other people who 'appeared' in my interview (e.g. my partner, friends); if I had used my real name, then information about them would have gone into the public domain without their consent, which may have caused distress.

Secondly, the Internet does reconfigure anonymity. However, if anything, the fact that research papers can now widely be disseminated way beyond the reach of academic journals means that using people's real names has far more potential for harm (e.g. if you took place as a named adolescent in research on emergent sexuality, you will be associated with this indefinitely and it may appear when a future employer or partner types your name in a search engine). The continued use of nicknames and online identities, as well as the taboo around 'outing' an online person in real-life, suggests that most people still value anonymity online, though not in all contexts.

Finally, at a practical level, negotiating anonymity and confidentiality on an individual basis with each participant or an entire organization/group is difficult. Not using anonymity may well be justified within, say, a long-term ethnographic study with a highly experienced researcher who has the time and energy to encourage critical reflection on the use of real names with participants. If this is the case, non-anonymity should be justified at the ethics review stage. In the vast majority of cases, anonymity is a reasonable default. One option, to give participants more ownership, is to offer them a choice of pseudonyms or ask them how they would like to be referred:

> *'We will not make use of your real name. We will need to refer to the organization to which you belong and your occupation. How would you like us to refer to you in our publications? (e.g. a manager, X-Corp)* _____

> Or

> *'We will not use your real name. This is to keep your data private and confidential. Please choose another name by which you would like to be known* _____ *'*

CONFIDENTIALITY

Confidentiality means not sharing the data after collection beyond agreed limits. Anonymity is a way of ensuring confidentiality, as the data is stored in an unidentifiable form. Confidentiality covers not only data protection and storage, but also how you, as the researcher, share the data in other ways, such as in conversation. It also covers how the data is shared between participants (e.g. in a group interview) or with external agencies (e.g. law enforcement, other authorities). In serious cases, confidentiality may be challenged if there are situations of harm (e.g. abuse or neglect) or because it been requested by law enforcement (e.g. if it contains disclosure of criminal activities). It is extremely important, therefore, that confidentiality should be agreed upfront as part of the consent agreement. This allows participants to make an informed choice about what they choose to share.

Legal and moral obligations

Confidentiality is a common practice within medicine, social work, psychology and other clinical settings. It allows the patient to speak freely, without fear of disclosure, unless this may cause serious harm to the person/others (e.g. threatening suicide or murder). Researchers do not necessarily have such professional obligations. In the UK, for example, there is no professional obligation on researchers to disclose serious information (except perhaps for terrorism activities). If the researcher is also a teacher, practicing psychologist, social worker or medic, their professional code may require disclosure. Researchers may also feel a moral obligation to intervene or disclose confidential material (e.g. confessions of illegal behaviour, abuse or of potential harm). In other jurisdictions, such as in the US, there are mandatory (state) requirements to report sexual abuse and elder abuse (Folkman, 2000, p. 52).

Another possible breach of confidentiality may occur if legal or law enforcement authorities require material to be handed over, for example, as part of an investigation into a crime or through requests during corporate litigation (Palys & Lowman, 2002). Generally, courts do not make these requests, upholding the principle of confidentiality of sources. There may be exceptions to this, for example, the Terrorism Act in the UK does not require permission for the seizure of research material.

You need to do some extra planning if you are researching in an area in which confidentiality may be a moral or legal problem. These might include the following:

● Research into illegal practices (e.g. drug addiction/use)
● Research with a group likely to have committed crimes ('at risk' teenagers or prisoners)
● Research with a group more likely to experience abuse/harm/ criminal acts (e.g. children in institutional settings, women, elder/older people)

Start by reading the relevant disciplinary guidelines and seek further advice from the ethics committee/IRB. There are several options to clarify and protect confidentiality, which still allow the possibility for disclosure in cases of severe harm:

1. *State if and when disclosure might occur:* To warn participants in the consent procedure that what they say may not be completely confidential, and that if anything illegal or harmful is discussed, you may have to inform someone else. This allows the participant to choose what to say. You might state something like:

   Everything you say will be kept confidential, in other words, I won't share it with other people. The only exception would be if you say something which makes us worry you or someone else will be harmed, in which case we would talk to you first about what to do next.

   The disadvantage of this approach is that from the outset, this positions you as part of an authority who may 'tell' which could jeopardize participant trust.

2. *Anonymize data*: Another option is to anonymize the data at source or immediately after collection, i.e. keep no record yourself of full names/addresses/other identifiers, thus limiting the potential for requests for disclosure.

3. *Use a certificate of confidentiality*: In the US, you can apply for this from the US Department of Health and Human Services and the US Department of Justice for certain types of eligible research (e.g. relating to drug use) (Folkman, 2000, p. 53).

Breaking confidentiality once the study has started is discussed further in Chapter 6. The key point is to seek advice initially from a supervisor/lead researcher or IRB/ethics officer. Minor issues can often be dealt with by encouraging the participant to seek help or discussing the dilemma with them. In serious cases, you need to seek further expertise.

Confidentiality within research teams

Most researchers are unlikely to have to disclose confidences such as abuse or criminal acts. However, confidentiality is still important in the day-to-day settings of research. It's about thinking before speaking about 'that crazy lady Bridget I went to interview'. It's about not leaving transcripts or digital recordings lying around with people's names on in a shared office.

It is also important, however, to be able to discuss ethical thinking and issues with other researchers. I called this 'ethical discussion' in Chapter 6. So, how does this need for 'ethical discussion' square with the need to maintain confidentiality? As I suggested in that chapter, one way to facilitate this sharing is to negotiate confidentiality between the participant and your 'research team' (even if this team is just you, your supervisor and transcriber). Where possible, it is better not to use names when discussing cases, but there are times in which you need to discuss a specific situation or participant. Similarly, you would not expect your doctor to share the confidential details of your medical history with his friends when drunk, but it is reasonable to expect them to be shared within a medical team to optimize care.

Here's an example statement you could use:

> *Everything you say will be kept confidential, in other words, I won't share it with other people, except those in my research team, so that means me and my supervisor, is that ok?*

Confidentiality within groups/communities

Another issue in confidentiality arises when researching with multiple participants/groups/families/communities. It is important to maintain confidentiality between interviews, for example, so not mentioning what one family member said to another. However, you cannot stop them recognizing each other in your findings. If this is the case, and complete confidentiality is unrealistic within the group or community you are working in, then it is better to be honest with participants. I am currently running a project interviewing families 'at risk' of Type 2 diabetes. I will adapt the consent form to explain the limits on confidentiality as follows:

> *Although I will not share your data with others and it won't have your name on it, it may be the case that you can recognize other people in your family and they can recognize you in the interviews, so do bear that in mind.*

DATA PROTECTION

Data storage

Many countries now have legislation which applies to the storage of personally identifiable data. Researchers cannot be sloppy about data storage because their participants have legal rights to access it and to have it stored securely. The days of keeping transcripts with names on in piles on a desk are well and truly over.

In the UK, data storage including research material is covered by the Data Protection Act (1998). This refers to all 'personal data', i.e. data with personally identifiable details. Personal details includes data such as names, addresses, national insurance/social security/ taxation details, specific employment details and other identifying digital data such as CCTV, audio and video files. If your data includes personal data, it must comply with a series of conditions: that it is legally processed in line with your rights, that it is used only for limited purposes, is adequate and relevant (i.e. not excessive), accurate and up to date, not kept for longer than necessary, secure and not transferred to other countries who don't have the same standards of data protection/without adequate protection. Once anonymized, data can be stored and used indefinitely for research purposes as it is exempt from the Act. This makes it important to anonymize the data as soon as possible for storage purposes.

Examples of good practice in data protection include the following:

- *Protecting data*: This might include storing personal data such as the identifier document (one containing the personal data removed for anonymization) in a locked cabinet or as an online password protected document.
- *Storing online data securely*: Many universities now have server systems in which data is stored in a secure online form. These can then be accessed from any computer in the world (a form of cloud computing). These can be more secure than storing data on a personal desktop or laptop. If data protection is a particular issue (e.g. you are working in a region where it is not advisable to carry participant data on your person), then uploading to a secure server may be a better option. Seek advice from IT services.
- *Not sending personal data by insecure means*: An example of insecure data transmission might be a name and address of a participant sent in the body of an email to another researcher.
- *Getting informed consent for data use*: This includes permission for things like re-interviewing or storing data in an archive at the time of the first interview.

An example sentence concerning data protection in a consent form might be:

> *We will store your data in accordance with the data protection legislation. This means we will keep it secure and destroy it after five years.*

Or

> *We will store your data in accordance with the data protection legislation. This means we will keep it indefinitely (forever) but not with your name or details on it.*

For a comprehensive list of data protection measures in the UK, see the Social Research Association/Market Research Association guidelines (Data Protection Act 1998: Guidelines for Social Research, SRA/MRA, 2005). The RESPECT EU project contains information on data protection relating to Europe. In Canada, researchers have to take account of The Personal Information Protection & Electronic Documents Act, 2000 as well as previous privacy legislation (Privacy Act, 1980). In Australia, data protection is covered by the Privacy Act 1988, and also the Privacy Amendment (Private Sector) Act, 2000. The US has no overarching data protection legislation, but a mixture of state/federal regulations. There is legislation for standards of privacy concerning individually identifiable health data, although researchers are exempt unless they are 'covered entities' (i.e. are doing work which is included in the Privacy Rule).

If you are working on a project which utilizes sensitive data (e.g. medical records), sending data between researchers or different countries, or matching different sets of personal data, you may need tailored IT/legal advice from the Data Protection Officer or IT department. Many institutions also run data protection workshops for researchers which are well worth attending.

Secondary data analysis

Secondary data is that which the researcher has not collected themselves. Examples include large-scale datasets from public health and cohort studies, medical records or archive data of different mediums (e.g. films, books, photographs, newspapers, diaries, public records). Many codes and IRB guidelines exempt secondary data analysis from full ethical review (e.g. in the US). This is because the rules of consent for data collection (i.e. the agreement between the participant and the researcher, if any) were already decided at the primary collection stage. The usual guidance, therefore, is to follow the rules set by the archive about their use. The ethical issues around secondary data use are also considered in the 'Methods' section in Chapter 4.

Archiving

Despite the potential benefits of archiving, it is not standard practice, particularly in qualitative research. This is a shame.

Collecting material, such as life history interviews, is often time-consuming. Allowing it to be used by others (secondary research) makes the most of existing data, for example, to be reanalysed, analysed for different content or comparative analyses to be conducted. Many funding bodies encourage data archiving of studies (e.g. the Economic and Social Research Council in the UK).

However, archiving does present ethical issues (Bishop, 2005; Corti & Thompson, 2003; Parry & Mauthner, 2004). Firstly, the ongoing relationship between researcher and participant in which the data was collected is no longer present. It is not possible to renegotiate privacy, anonymity or confidentiality, or indeed the material being archived, at this stage. Secondly, it may be difficult for people to anticipate the range of potential future uses of their data at the original consent stage. Finally, unlike in oral history, much social science research deposited in archives has been stripped of personal identifiers, including places and employment details. This can make subsequent qualitative analysis, which depends on a nuanced understanding of context and meanings, problematic. If you think archiving might be appropriate for your study or it is required by the funding body, seek advice from the archivists about collection and preparation of material; participant consent would also need to include consent to archive from the outset.

SUMMARY

As with informed consent, practices around privacy, anonymity and confidentiality have become standardized within social research; however, they remain the subject of some debate. The key to departing from standardization is to understand why you are doing so, and ensure that alternative practices are equally ethical. The next chapter considers practices around another standard feature of ethical review: the assessment of possible harms.

CASE STUDY: AN INVASION OF PRIVACY

A postgraduate student in our institution was becoming very anxious about falling behind, so, with many interviews left to transcribe, asked one of his friends to help. The student did think about confidentiality and anonymity to the extent that he had ensured that the label on the recording was anonymous. However, as his friend started transcribing, he recognized the voice on it as someone he knew, talking about quite personal issues and experiences in their life. Despite this, he carried on transcribing. When I heard about this incident, I was quite shocked. This was not just a breach of anonymity and confidentiality (although arguably it was both), it was an invasion of privacy. The participant, who had talked in good faith, expecting full confidentiality, had had their personal life and private opinions exposed to someone they saw every day. For this reason, many codes and guidelines suggest using only certified transcribers or transcribing interviews yourself to prevent privacy (and data protection) breaches.

Ethical Dilemma 8: Challenging anonymity as the norm

Dave has just started his research project looking at coping strategies of people living with HIV. He is planning to interview a small sample of five people at least two or three times each. As the research is for his master's dissertation, he has no current plans to publish the results, but this may change as he is thinking of continuing a career in research. He has recruited his participants through a local support group through a contact. It was difficult to find participants who wanted to be interviewed in the first place, so he stressed that all interview data would be completely confidential and anonymous. However, at the first meeting with one participant, they were adamant that they wanted their name to be used, 'because this is part of who I am'. Dave is now unsure whether to return to his original ethics proposal and ask whether removing anonymity could be an option.

1. What do you suggest Dave do?
2. What are the advantages and disadvantages of using people's real names? Which of these are ethical reasons?
3. Should anonymity remain the 'default setting' in research?

---

9 Assessment of Possible Harm

Assessment of possible harms and benefits is undertaken before a project starts so that the participants can be fully informed about them, and for them to be modified if they are ethically unacceptable. As I discussed in Chapter 5, the section in ethics proposals covering assessment of possible harm/risks is often a problematic area, because researchers find it difficult to pitch the level of harm/ risk correctly. This chapter looks at what is meant by 'risk', 'harm', 'minimal risk' and 'benefits' for the purposes of ethical review. It then looks at the major types of risk for participants/participating organizations and considers practical solutions for managing them. Researcher safety, an often overlooked risk in research projects, is also discussed.

WHAT IS 'HARM' AND 'RISK'?

In this context, 'harm' has a specific meaning, which is a detrimental occurrence, or negative outcome. Assessment of possible harms is therefore the assessment of negative outcomes which may occur to participants, communities or even to society at large as the result of a given piece of research. 'Risk' is another term which is often used interchangeably with 'harm'; it includes the notion of likelihood (i.e. the risk is the likelihood a certain harm will occur). The use of the term 'harm' stems from medical research where there may be a physical risk of harm to the patient or even death (e.g. in early clinical trials or new surgical procedures). However, in most social science research, participants are unlikely to be physically harmed in this sense.

HOW CAN YOU ASSESS 'HARM' AND 'RISK'?

It is difficult to assess harm/risks for several reasons. Firstly, it is a predictive activity in which you essentially guess some of the likely outcomes of your research. My experience is that although some ethical issues that arise are quite predictable (e.g. if you are doing a project involving institutional care for children, then issues concerning power and potential abuse are moderately likely to arise), others catch you by surprise. Secondly, although many codes and federal regulations require the balance of 'risks' and 'benefits' (i.e. so that a more risky project needs to have greater benefits to outweigh the negatives), there is no formula for this. It is simply a matter of perception. Thirdly, risks/harms differ dramatically in their severity. In some studies, the chances of anything very bad happening are very low, but the potential harm is very great (e.g. being attacked, put in prison, having severe side-effects from medication). This might be weighed differently than a study in which the harm is not that great (e.g. being a little distressed by a topic) but is likely to occur to a significant proportion of the study population. Finally, not all risks/harms apply to all participants in any given study. What may be perceived as 'harm' by one participant (e.g. experiencing an interview as an invasion of privacy) may be a 'benefit' to another (e.g. a welcome opportunity to talk) (Sieber, 2000).

'Minimal risk' is a category into which much social science research falls. The advantage of having a project classified as 'minimal risk' is that it may not have to undergo full review; it may also give flexibility over, for example, using alternative consent procedures. However, it is up to the IRB/committee to decide how to operationalize the 'minimal risk' classification. Sometimes there may be a disparity between the reseacher's understanding of the risk of a project and that of the IRB/committee. For more on 'minimal risk' and ethical review procedures, see Chapter 3.

Risks or harms are assessed against a set of criterion which may include the following:

- Is the risk/harm normally encountered by participants in their everyday lives?
- Is the risk/harm likely to be short-lived or have longer term consequences?

- Is the risk/harm likely to cause more than minimal distress/discomfort?
- Is the risk/harm proportionate (e.g. in balance with the benefits of the project)?
- Are there risks/harms associated with the participant group? (i.e. are they vulnerable subjects such as minority or stigmatized groups/children/institutionalized?)

Some of these criteria have been criticized. For example, there are groups of people who live more difficult or violent or risky lives. However, it is far from clear that it is ethical to expose them to greater risks as a result of this misfortune than those with comfortable lives just because it is normal for them.

PHYSICAL, PSYCHOLOGICAL OR EMOTIONAL HARM

Physical harm/risk

It is not true that physical risk is never an issue in social science; projects sometimes involve physical discomfort or potential safety issues for participants. However, the vast majority of social research, particularly student projects, does not fall into that category, which is why it is best to seek extra advice if your research is 'higher risk' in this sense.

Example: Discomfort as part of an experiment

Topic: *A third-year researcher is working with his supervisor to study the effects of discomfort on working memory. The experiment involves participants plunging their hands into a bucket of freezing water whilst reciting some previously remembered number sequences.*

Management of risk: *It is likely that the participants will feel some discomfort (that's the point of the study) but as long as the experimenter makes it very clear they can remove their hand if it becomes too uncomfortable, and they can stop at any time, there are not likely to be long-term consequences of taking part.*

143

Example: Researching with individuals living with domestic violence

Topic: *A post-doctoral student is working on a funded study interviewing women and men living currently in situations of domestic violence. This could be potentially risky if their abusive partner discovered their participation.*

Management of risk: *Working with this participant group to design a safe study from the outset would be paramount (e.g. talking with domestic abuse charities, advisors or focus groups with users). Issues would include how to manage contact/interviews with participants in a safe space and data protection to preserve complete confidentiality and anonymity.*

Psychological/emotional harm

This is probably one of the most common risks in social research. This might include distress, upset, annoyance, emotional dependence on researcher, misunderstanding the nature of the relationship, provoking negative memories/flashbacks/mental health issues or any other negative aspect of psychological interaction.

Research into certain topics, such as sensitive issues and/or research with vulnerable populations (e.g. those with mental health problems, learning disabled, vulnerable children or adults), is more likely to present physical or psychological risk to participants (see the Hot Topic 'Vulnerable Groups and Sensitive Topics', Chapter 10). Other risks may occur because of a breach of confidentiality or privacy, which may cause considerable distress.

Research interactions such as interviews or surveys may also cause emotional experiences such as crying/distress/feeling upset/embarrassment or a sense of intrusion. This is not limited to sensitive topics. Even quite bland seeming areas can make people cry. A topic like health, money, lifestyles, relationships, children, hobbies, even talking to participants about their choice of car are not neutral, but is interwoven with people's experiences of life, good and bad. It is natural that sometimes they become upset. Someone may confess something they don't tell very often. Or talking about the topic may have reminded them of a loved one, or a difficult time in their lives. As Holloway and Jefferson argue, consent isn't just a cognitive decision, it's a decision about emotions, whether and how much to share (Holloway & Jefferson, 2000). Some researchers choose to share back their own experiences, so that the exchange of information (and the power balance) is more even (see Chapter 6 for more on how to handle distress).

Example: Interviewing people about their risk of breast cancer

Issue: *A PhD student is conducting interviews with women under 40 who are being tested for the BRCA gene, which is linked with much higher rates of breast cancer. All the women come from families in which there is a history of breast cancer and in which close relatives may have died.*

Management of risk: *This student is working with clinicians/ consultants within existing health care pathways so is able to offer access to support such as genetic counselling. She also has a strategy in place for dealing with distress in interviews.*

ECONOMIC, REPUTATIONAL OR LEGAL HARM

Students and researchers often forget to identify these as risks. This is a mistake as these are common areas for disputes to break out, for example, after a thesis is handed in and a company or individual named in it feel their reputation has been maligned in some way. I have even known an academic demand a right to reply to part of a PhD thesis, which they felt misrepresented their work and the dispute continued on into publications for some years.

Commercial/economic harm

Commercial risk relates to the issues that can arise for companies or organizations, particularly if confidentiality or anonymity is breached. Many companies fear that internal information about products or processes might pass to other companies during research, or into the public domain. They may also worry that their company may be harmed by adverse publicity, for example, if an evaluative study showed their product or service to be ineffective or detrimental.

Example: A case study of a company using new fuel technologies

Issue: *A master's student is doing a case study in business studies evaluating the management strategy of a company using new fuel technologies, interviewing several staff members. Although the company has provisionally agreed to participate, they are worried about being identified as their product is unique on the market.*

Management of risk: *Clarifying how the participants will be identified, both at the level of the company and the individuals, is vital, as is a clear agreement about what aspects of the technology will be mentioned and what kept confidential.*

Reputational risk

Individuals, organizations and communities can be concerned about their reputations or even dispute findings or the way they are characterized in research. Reputational risk can occur in several scenarios: to public or identifiable figures (e.g. if their verbatim quotes lead to reputational or political damage), to societies or communities (e.g. one of the debates about the ethics of the anthropological research with the Yamomamo tribe discussed in Chapter 1 was the reputational damage of identifying them as the 'fierce people') or to institutions (e.g. if a research attracts the 'wrong type' of publicity). Minimizing reputational risk (e.g. by giving the participants or institution the right to veto any outputs) can come into conflict with other ethical principles, namely academic freedom. Again, having a robust consent procedure at the start of research, including discussion of confidentiality, anonymity and outputs, is very important in minimizing these risks.

Example: Political interviews with former heads of state of failed regimes

Issue: *A PhD student has access through personal contacts to the former head of state and government minster of a failed regime. Although the interviewees are keen to participate, they are not keen to sign anything.*

Management of risk: *There may be political, reputational as well as safety issues with this project. For this reason, it is important to negotiate consent transparently, including whether these interviews are 'on' or 'off the record' and whether verbatim quotes can be used. Checking back with the interviewees before publication may also offer greater security for them and encourage openness.*

Legal risks

Legal risks include participants being investigated, arrested or prosecuted for something illegal disclosed during interviews (e.g. criminal acts, drug use, terrorism) or captured on film or being sued for something published in research (e.g. that was libellous). These risks primarily relate to how anonymity, confidentiality and privacy are handled, particularly in 'high risk' projects with legal dimensions. The various ways of protecting participant identities and managing the risk of enforced disclosure are discussed in detail in the Hot Topic, Privacy, Anonymity and Confidentiality (Chapter 8).

Example: Addiction research with long-term drug users

Issue: *A project looking at the intervention needs for long-term drug users is being run by a team of research assistants and post-docs working for a well-known professor of addiction. The research involves ethnographic observation and interviews over a period of a year.*

Management of risks: *Participation requires considerable trust and long-term relationships to be built; otherwise the project will not go ahead. A participatory model is selected which involves groups from this particular community in designing, running and disseminating the outputs. Options include: getting a 'certificate of confidentiality' for the project, working with local law enforcement to educate them about benefits of the project and/or setting out the legal boundaries for participants before interviewing them.*

Example: Project on alcohol/prescription drug use in the student population

Issue: *A master's student is doing a three-month study interviewing other students about their use of alcohol and prescription drugs. Students may not limit themselves to discussing legal drugs.*

Management of risk: *No data identifying the participants will be collected by the researcher, who will interview the participants only once, and give them a designated number.*

The tolerance of risk by IRBs/committees or other institutional mechanisms is very much a function of the level of experience of the researcher. Many institutions will expect practice or student research to be lower risk for this reason; higher risk projects demand greater expertise.

An example of an assessment of harms section for a minimal risk project is included in Chapter 5.

BENEFITS OF PARTICIPATION (BENEFICENCE)

Beneficence, or 'benefitting others', is a key ethical principle contained in the Belmont Code. Beneficence is part of equation that IRBs and ethics committees take account of when considering assessment of possible harm. The aim is to balance the risks of participation against the benefits in a way that is 'reasonable' (Federal Regulation 45 CRF 46.111). But what is a 'benefit' in this context, and how can these be balanced against risks or potential harm?

Some comprehensive lists have been made of all the possible 'benefits'. Sieber has created a matrix with seven major categories of benefit for a community: (1) valuable relationships, (2) knowledge or education, (3) material resources, (4) training, employment, opportunity for advancement, (5) opportunity to do good and receive the esteem of others, (6) empowerment (personal, political) and (7) scientific/ clinical outcomes (Sieber, 2000, p. 99). She goes on to specify how these categories might apply to relationships with seven actors: subjects, community, researcher, institution, funder, science and society. This creates 49 potential types of benefit. Considering benefits through such a matrix may be appropriate for larger-scale, long-term or community/participatory projects. However (as Sieber herself points out), for many students such as master's or doing student projects, such benefits either to the community under study, or to wider scientific knowledge are unrealistic. So, how can we conceptualize 'benefits' in a simplified but thorough way?

I think of benefits in terms of three levels:

1. Benefit to participants.

These are the direct benefits that may accrue to participants as a result of participating. These might include things such as (a) increased knowledge about a particular area, topic or intervention; (b) increased self-esteem from participating; (c) the opportunity to tell one's story or express opinions/attitudes which might be cathartic/validating/means of being heard; (d) the opportunity to live according to one's values (e.g. concerning participation or taking part in research); and (e) the opportunity to potentially contribute to change. Payment, discussed in Chapter 4, also counts as a direct benefit.

Examples of increasing participant benefit: giving participants information/leaflets/website access to the literature on the study, preparing a short user-friendly report of outputs, thanking participants genuinely, using participatory methods to incorporate participants' ideas into the design and running of the study, disseminating the study outputs to, and working with, those who can effect change (e.g. policymakers).

2. Benefit to group/community/institution

As discussed in Chapter 2, many researchers aim to effect social change and champion social justice through research with groups and communities. In such research, the potential 'benefits' to the group or community are high; although any IRB/ethics committee will expect to see details of how these goals will be achieved in practice rather than stated as an ideal. These might include (a) improved relationships between the community/researchers/ funders and institutions; (b) increased community awareness and empowerment regarding the issue at hand; (c) increased self-esteem and positive identity for community as contributor; (d) increased access to material resources (e.g. intervention/training programmes or material goods); and (e) benefit of increased scientific knowledge about the community. However, not all community or organizational projects fit within this type of model. If you are proposing research within a company or a health care provider or science lab then specifying the particular benefit to that institution may be harder. It may be the opportunity to learn more about themselves from another perspective and/or it accords with the institution's values in terms of participating in valuable projects.

Examples of increasing community benefit: Using participant focus groups or community meetings to generate initial research questions; doing feedback meetings to communities/groups/ institutions about how the study is running/their response to it, disseminating results throughout the community in ways that maximize the potential social change possible (e.g. inviting key gatekeepers/policy-makers).

3. Benefit to wider society and scientific knowledge

Hammersley makes the very important point that in some ways, the most beneficial (and ethically justifiable) thing you can offer to participants is to conduct very high-quality research (Hammersley, 1999). This in turn may contribute to the larger body of scientific knowledge, and/or policy arenas. These might include (a) filling a knowledge 'gap', adding weight to existing theories or proposing new ones, (b) providing evidence for evidence-based practice, (c) contributing to policy development and (d) contributing to political, economic or social change.

But most student (or even staff) research does not, at the level of an individual piece of research, make a very substantive impact on the state of knowledge or policy. So does that mean it is not worth doing at all? One reason for students to undertake small projects is to have more research literate population. It also trains the next generation of researchers. It is also beneficial to have a society which encourages participation and values social research. However, individual researchers should not make unrealistic claims about their likely societal/scientific impact.

Examples of increasing scientific knowledge: Doing high-quality research which meets recognized quality criteria (e.g. valid, reliable, transparent, plausible), writing publications in peer-reviewed journals, disseminating beyond academic boundaries (e.g. to user group, clinicians or policy-makers) and in a wide variety of formats (e.g. workshops, online groups).

Higher risk projects will, given the risk/benefit ratio, require greater potential benefits. For example, IRBs and ethics committees may require evidence of the quality of proposed research, such as external peer review of protocols.

Although ethical codes tend to specify 'beneficience' in terms of benefit to participants, others also benefit from conducting research, such as institutions (universities, centres), funders and researchers themselves. Individual researchers benefit in terms of developing their career, bolstering their reputation and in financial terms. Although this is not usually discussed in formal ethical review, the benefits of other actors need to be considered when asking 'who benefits?'

Finally, people may misunderstand what their personal benefit is from participation. People often think I am a health professional, particularly if the study is conducted through a local health care centre, so think I will be able to advise them on their health problems. I now clearly state I am a researcher, so not able to offer advice, and redirect them towards sources of help. Nyambedha (2008) reports that when doing ethnographic research with orphans in Western Kenya, participants perceived participation would result in the children being taken care of by the researchers, which was not the case. Although most research projects do not involve such tragic hopes and expectations on the part of participants, participants may not understand what being involved means for them. This is why a clear explanation, on the information sheet or in person to the community, of the benefits of research is necessary to clarify everyone's expectations.

IS THE NOTION OF HARM APPROPRIATE?

Most researchers and students reading this book will not be doing research which is likely to greatly harm their participants (or at least I hope not!) Indeed, it has been argued that it is wrong to apply the very strict criterion of medical ethics, in which there may be a small but significant risk of harm or even death, to social research (Dingwall, 2006; Jacobsen et al., 2007). Although some criticism of the risk-averse nature of IRBs/ethics committees is undoubtedly justified, I do not find this an entirely compelling argument. Firstly, as discussed in Chapter 1, the case of the Yamomamo anthropological studies has shown that social scientists can be accused of harm of great magnitude (e.g. sexual abuse, introducing disease to a virgin population) (Tierney, 2000). Secondly, medics are not cavalier about the risks of research. The death or disability of a subject in clinical trials is also very rare and would trigger a major clinical and legal investigation (Hedgecoe, 2008b). Thirdly, most social research does not come anywhere near the same level of ethical scrutiny as bringing a drug to market, which can take up to 10 years.

Harms such as upsetting or distressing participants, invading privacy, maligning reputations or causing social damage within a community may be minor in comparison to death (what isn't?), but their accumulatory effect is to devalue social research as a professional enterprise. It is not abandoning the concept of 'harm' or 'risk' altogether, which will benefit social research, but the inclusion of more social researchers in ethics review procedures so that the mainly small but accumulative harms can be realistically assessed and managed.

Quick question

How do you keep yourself safe (e.g. when out with friends, in large cities, meeting someone you don't know)? How might these strategies be useful for increasing researcher safety?

RESEARCHER SAFETY

Much research takes the researcher out of their own environment and into others, which vary in terms of safety. Just as you can never exclude the possibility that a participant might be harmed by your research, you can never exclude the possibility that you, the researcher, might be harmed. Researcher safety is often neglected in formal ethical review.

Own response to research

Researchers and students are first and foremost human beings like their research subjects. This means that on occasions, particularly if researching a sensitive subject or one personal to the researcher, they may find themselves upset, distressed or even angry.

The way to cope with researcher stress or distress will vary just as it would with a participant, depending on the depth of the experience. Many mentors or supervisors understand that researchers need to 'debrief' after interviews or in a longer-term observation study and will offer that opportunity to talk through the experience. Talking with others in the same position or having similar experiences (whilst not breaking participant confidentiality) is another way of de-stressing. Many researchers keep a diary of their experiences during a project alongside their 'official' field notes or data. This can act as a safety valve for emotional experiences; it also adds context and self-reflexive thoughts to the overall data collection that can be useful for interpretation or if you intend to incorporate personal reflections when writing up.

Safety

Researcher safety means anticipating potential risks to yourself (and other members of your research team) and putting in place strategies to manage those risks. The extent to which individuals can take responsibility for assessing and managing their own safety differs depending on experience. The more experienced researcher may have greater knowledge of how to wriggle out of difficult situations, and what to do if they arise. Students, at both undergraduate and postgraduate level, may require more help in assessing their levels of personal risk and training in simple strategies to manage them.

Risks to the researcher, like risks to participants, can be of different types. Researching with human subjects puts us in contact with people who may have their own problems which are not necessarily apparent when they sign up to take part in an experiment or be interviewed.

For lone research, common-sense precautions apply here, just as they would if you were to go to meet a stranger for a date. Inviting participants to come to the university, laboratory or college, or meeting in a public space (e.g. café) is safer than meeting people in their own homes. However, there can be a strong motivation to conduct research on people's own territories, as they might be likely to be more relaxed. If this is the case, then one strategy is to let a supervisor or colleague know where you are, who you are with, what time you will return and your mobile number through a quick email. If the supervisor or colleague is not keen to get involved in the day-to-day movements of their students (and some aren't), then I would let a friend or family member know where you are, without breaking confidentiality.

Another strategy for improving researcher safety is to team up with another lone researcher. I knew a pair of students (one male, one female) who were doing separate research projects into the geography of social deprivation. This involved visiting deprived areas/districts in which crime and drug use were high. They had to interview in the evenings, which were dark in winter, as many participants were working in the daytime. After swapping scary experiences after the first few interviews, more with the local youths than with the participants they were visiting, they agreed to accompany each other to the interviews. One interviewed, whilst the other either came in or waited outside. They also considered how they appeared to others, for example, they also dressed down so as not to draw attention to themselves as 'outsiders'. It did take them longer to collect the data by teaming up. However, it was clear that interviewing one-to-one in this setting was a risk to their safety, and that they had to have a strategy in place.

Dealing with difficult or aggressive participants

Even if your antenna hasn't signalled an issue prior to starting the research, there is always a small chance that something may go wrong during the data collection. One issue is how to handle participants who suddenly become difficult or even aggressive in an interview situation. One key strategy is to trust your instincts. If someone turns up and seems threatening or difficult in some way from the start, there is no need to be polite and not listen to that instinct. If I were conducting interviews on campus, for example, I would always leave the door open and make it clear that colleagues were around, just as I would if a student came to talk. I have also said no to someone who suggested a further interview in a more remote location and was quite insistent. Perhaps my instincts were wrong, but you can always get another participant. No one participant is that crucial that it is worth risking your own safety.

During an interview or observation situation, very occasionally people can get defensive or even aggressive. This is more likely if you are working with higher risk populations or with vulnerable subjects (e.g. people with certain addictions) but could happen in what seems like just a regular interview. If it is the topic which appears to be causing them to get defensive, you could either switch onto a more neutral topic or suggest taking a break. Sometimes showing empathy to the cause of their stress (whilst maintaining your own safety) is more appropriate, if their defensiveness or anger is about frustrating situations in their lives. If it appears that there is another reason why they are behaving erratically, or they actually become physically aggressive, then you should do what you would do if you were in any such situation in your everyday life and get out of it quickly and sensibly.

Risky topics

It is also possible that researchers and students are drawn to particular topics precisely because they are a bit 'risky' or 'deviant'. This is natural. Researchers are human and often attracted to find out about those who are not like them (the 'other' in sociological terms), or to have experiences they would otherwise not have. For example, an older middle-class researcher might be intrigued by street culture as a topic and try to gain access and acceptance into a young gang. However, it is a very naïve researcher that doesn't consider the risks of such research and try to mitigate them.

In other research studies, the location is inherently more risky. This includes researching with vulnerable groups living in dangerous or impoverished structural environments, or engaging in risky behaviours (see Chapter 10). Often institutions will ask you to fill in a risk assessment as part of your insurance for doing research, which includes how you will assess the risk to yourself. Again, this is about risk management. Strategies include: taking local advice from people on the ground, contacting your consulate or Foreign Office and following their guidelines, and good data security (e.g. not keeping compromising material on you). The last is particularly important. One student doing research in the Occupied Territories found it safer to upload the data every few days onto a university server, or email host, rather than carry lists of names and addresses on their personal laptop.

In conclusion, there's no point in over-estimating the harm that could come to you by carrying out your research. Plenty of the activities we do when researching, such as talking with strangers, being on our own with people, observing people in public places or asking someone to fill in a survey, are things that we do in everyday life or other lines of work and not 'special' to research. Nevertheless, thinking critically about researcher safety is an important part of being an 'ethical researcher' and one that should not be neglected.

SUMMARY

Assessment of possible harm and benefit is an inexact science, given that it requires the researcher to predict likely outcomes which can be difficult to foresee, and which will be weighed differently by different actors. The aim should be to offer a realistic picture of a likely set of risks/benefits, which is neither exaggerated nor minimized. Dimensions of 'harm/risk' include: severity, typicality (in everyday life), longevity and proportionality (i.e. balanced against the benefits). Particular risks feature in research with vulnerable groups. Ways of assessing potential risks to participants include discussing them with participant groups or other researchers, or examining similar projects/examples. Official levels of risk (e.g. minimal, level I, II and III) should be checked with the individual IRB/ethics committee before application. In terms of researcher safety, again, not overestimating the harm that could come to you is important, as is having sensible practical strategies in place to mitigate any risks.

Ethical Dilemma 9: Balancing keeping safe against other risks

Cora is researching how people utilize and think about energy (e.g. fuel of different types) in their households using semi-structured interviews. Mindful of the need to keep safe, she has tried conducting interviews in public places, but she has often found them very noisy and she finds it hard to interview when people are watching. Several participants have suggested she visit their houses to do the interviews, but she is concerned about being in a lone researcher situation. When she spoke with her supervisor, he was rather cavalier about this and told her not to worry about it too much and use her 'common sense'. His attitude is that taking risks is all part of being a researcher and tells stories about the days in which he narrowly escaped being beaten up several times by the drug dealers he was interviewing.

1. Which types of research are likely to increase researcher safety risks?
2. What steps could Cora take to increase her safety as a researcher in this project?
3. Is worrying about researcher safety a sign of a risk management culture 'gone mad' or an important aspect of research ethics?

---

10 Vulnerable Groups and Sensitive Topics

This 'Hot Topic' chapter looks at two types of research which require extra ethical attention: research with vulnerable groups and sensitive topics. Such research is usually designated as 'higher risk' (i.e. more than minimal risk) for the purposes of formal ethical review. IRBs/ethics committees will usually require full review and greater scrutiny of proposals meeting these definitions. This chapter covers what constitutes a 'vulnerable group' or 'sensitive topic' and looks at some issues, in particular how to design consent procedures for vulnerable groups and how to manage privacy/confidentiality issues for sensitive topics. It also considers whether the designation of vulnerable groups or sensitive topics is always a 'good thing' from an ethical perspective.

Quick question

Is it helpful to think of groups such as women from ethnic minority groups, or people with disabilities, as 'vulnerable'? Why or why not?

WHAT IS A 'VULNERABLE GROUP'?

The identification of vulnerable groups stems from the historic mistreatment in research of disadvantaged and institutionalized groups such as the learning disabled, mentally ill, prisoners and military personnel (see Chapter 1).

Participants may be considered vulnerable for the following reasons (note: some participants may be multiply vulnerable):

1. *Institutionalized groups.* This includes people living in enclosed groups or institutions of any type, such as those in the care of

the state (e.g. children's homes, hostels), those who are incarcerated (e.g. in prisons, young offender institutes or on probation) and those who live in institutions (e.g. those who are hospitalized, in hospices, in mental health wards/institutions or living supervised in the community).

2. *Groups with issues over capacity to consent* (also see Chapter 7). This could include temporary issues with capacity (e.g. during an episode of acute mental illness) or through disability or injury (e.g. people with learning disabilities, Alzheimer's or dementia, stroke, brain tumour). It might also include enclosed groups with strong hierarchical organization such as the military, law enforcement or even schools and workplaces where voluntariness is an issue.

3. *Traditionally marginalized, disadvantaged or stigmatized groups.* These could include women in general, pregnant women, minority religious or ethnic groups, stigmatized groups (e.g. through ethnicity/race, class, poverty, sexuality, age, health status such as having HIV/AIDS or immigration status such as illegal workers or asylum seekers), those with psychiatric disorders; those with disabilities (learning disabilities and/or physical impairments). It also includes minors/children under 18 (see the next 'Hot Topic'). Note, I say 'traditionally marginalized' as it is possible that members of these groups have positive self-identities and many may not individually be 'vulnerable'.

4. *Groups living in dangerous or impoverished structural environments, or engaging in risky behaviours.* This might include: people living in war zones, people with addictions (e.g. illegal drugs, alcoholism), people who are homeless or temporarily housed, people living in poverty, people with restricted access to basic resources (e.g. disease, fuel, shelter, water) or in developing countries with poor infrastructure, people engaged in violence/acts or war/acts of criminality, people who are being abused (physically, mentally or emotionally). These research environments are also likely to be risky for the researcher.

There are two main features which distinguish 'vulnerable groups'. One is that they typically stand in a differential power relation with the researcher than others in the general population. Researchers are typically associated with powerful institutions (e.g. funders, universities). They are also often from more advantaged groups (e.g. high educational level, higher socio-economic status or different ethnicity) than the groups studied. People in less powerful groups may be susceptible to participating in research for economic reasons or as an act of compliance, find it harder to assert their right to privacy, and so on. Furthermore, it has been argued some research actively keeps participants 'vulnerable', for example, if it evaluates existing repressive institutions (e.g. Hunt, 1981). Participatory and transformative approaches have emerged as part of an ethical critique of paternalistic top-down research, particularly with vulnerable groups (e.g. Ferguson, 1993; Wilkinson, 2002). They suggest rebalancing the power differential by giving all participants a more equitable role within the research process.

Secondly, vulnerable groups are often only accessed through 'gatekeepers' (e.g. children through adults such as headteachers; people with psychiatric disorders through consultants; military personnel through the military hierarchy). Even user groups and charities are often facilitated by individuals in charge. This can cause difficulties if the ethical needs of participants (e.g. to maintain privacy) potentially clash with the desire of gatekeepers who may have their own motivations for participation (see also 'Hot Topic: Informed Consent' (Chapter 7) on webs of consent).

However, the possible ethical difficulties of research with vulnerable groups have to be weighed against the potential benefits of research. Research may given insight or offer solutions for a relevant problem; offer the chance to evaluate a useful intervention, or give a vulnerable group a political presence; in other words, an opportunity to redress their vulnerability. Although some groups have ended up over-researched due to their vulnerability, some have ended up under-researched. For example, the Alzheimer's Society in the UK has a campaign for more research with people living with Alzheimer's. They are often excluded from research because they are perceived as a 'difficult' group from which to gain consent and researchers anticipate problems with IRBs/ethics committees.

The designation of 'vulnerable groups' as a distinct category for the purposes of research ethics has been questioned (e.g. Melrose, 2011). It automatically classifies the group as needy and/or inherently problematic. This can be seen as a disempowering and disenfranchising designation. It also suggests that it is an inherent aspect of their group/individual status which renders them vulnerable. Social models of disability hold that it is society which is structured to exclude all abilities (classifying them as 'disabled' or 'impaired'). Studying disabled individuals as a 'disadvantaged group' may perpetuate traditional negative assumptions about them and ignore the social causes of disability (Barnes & Mercer, 2003; Oliver, 1992). Other groups simply categorize themselves as part of the diversity of humanity rather than 'vulnerable' (e.g. autism or deaf community activists).

VULNERABLE PARTICIPANTS AND CONSENT

Researching with vulnerable groups requires the researcher to think more reflexively about how consent is going to work in practice. The issues with informed consent can be divided into three broad categories:

1. *Problems with the ability to retain information and understand it.* Reasons include impaired memory, limited intellectual capacity, limited reading skills or problems with decision-making. This could be something that is inherent to being a group member (e.g. people with learning disabilities or who have had a stroke/Alzheimer's disease) or lifestyle/environmental factors (e.g. drug use/chaotic lives).
2. *Problems with voluntariness.* This is particularly problematic in institutional settings such as care homes or hospitals where there is a restriction of independent decision-making (Ellis, 1992), or where the researcher is positioned in a dual role as a carer/professional/friend (Thompson, 2002).
3. *Problems with communicating consent.* Some members of vulnerable groups have communication and language differences (e.g. due to a stroke, using minority languages or non-verbal signs), which make a typical written consent form inappropriate.

Capacity to consent is a legal term, which relates to 'competence'. In the UK, research with participants with an impaired/no capacity to consent is specifically covered in the Mental Capacity Act 2005. There are several aspects to competence: being able to understand, retain and weigh up information; and communicate the decision by any means possible, including talking, sign language or behaviour such as blinking or squeezing a hand.

In the UK, research involving participants with impaired or no capacity to consent has to be reviewed by an NHS committee, not a university one. However, just because some people in a vulnerable group might have impaired capacity to consent, does not mean all of them will. Indeed, mental capacity legislation presumes that all patients are legally competent unless there is evidence otherwise (HMSO, 2005; Rozovsky, 1997). This means that research with people with learning disabilities, mental health problems or conditions such as strokes or Alzheimer's needs should not be excluded on the basis of difficulties with consent. Furthermore, there is an increasing trend to consent participants themselves in these group, rather than rely on 'proxy consent' (e.g. by carers, nurses) as in the past (Wilkinson, 2002).

QUESTIONS TO CONSIDER FOR INFORMED CONSENT WITH VULNERABLE GROUPS

1. *If there are issues around capacity to consent*, you need to consider (a) how will this capacity be assessed, by whom and does anyone need training? (b) how often will capacity be assessed (e.g. at the start of every session, during each session); (c) how will participants indicate they want to participate or withdraw (e.g. will they sign a written consent, use verbal consent, give a sign or other indication)?
2. *If there are issues around comprehension and understanding*, you will need to consider (a) how should the materials be presented (e.g. in visual form, using which language)? (b) how can comprehension and understanding be enhanced (e.g. in group discussions of participation, in meetings of residents)?
3. *If there are issues around voluntariness*, you will need to consider (a) how have the needs and pressures on participants been established and managed (e.g. need for friendship, need to please gatekeepers or researchers)?

For example, if you want to do a project with patients in the early stages of dementia, designing consent procedures might include contacting the relevant NGOs/charities, reading the relevant legislation on mental capacity in your country, and asking researchers already working in the area how they handle informed consent. You might then devise a consent procedure which takes account of the fluctuating nature of ability to consent (between different individuals and within one individual across time) and pilot it with a user group.

WHAT IS A SENSITIVE TOPIC?

'Sensitive topics' is also a designation used within formal ethical review to identify types of research which are particularly ethically problematic, often in terms of privacy issues. Sensitive topics can either be considered intrinsically 'sensitive' (i.e. in most situations) such as researching sexuality, or 'sensitive' in a context. Sieber gives the example of asking Catholic communities about HIV (Sieber, 2000).

The designation of sensitive topics is typically used for topics which are either

1. *not part of everyday discourse or are taboo or stigmatized*: This includes sexual practices, sexuality in general, abusive behaviour of all kinds, prejudiced behaviour of all kinds, particular types of health issue such as HIV/AIDS, disfigurement or impairment;
2. *criminal or illegal activities*, e.g. prostitution/sex work, drug use, criminal activities, terrorist activities, all types of fraud or tax evasion, begging, also research on the boundaries around these activities (quasi-legal); or
3. *personal topics which may cause distress*, such as death, illness, health problems or ageing, experiences of abuse, racism, sexism and so on.

Research with already 'vulnerable groups' can also take place on 'sensitive topics', amplifying the ethical issues further. An example of this would be research on the sexuality of disabled people (Shakespeare, 1997).

This is not an exhaustive list, and the designation of 'sensitivity' is subjective. However, what they have in common is that the topics are not necessarily part of everyday talk or public display (although they might be for participants) and so raise issues concerning privacy and intrusion into people's lives, as well as potential problems for those who participate in research about them (e.g. increasing stigmatization or being seen as colluding). For more on how to secure privacy with sensitive topics, see 'Hot Topic: Privacy, Anonymity and Confidentiality' (Chapter 8). Sensitive topics may also be distressing (see Chapter 6 for strategies to manage distress).

It has been argued that designating some research as 'sensitive' may be counter-productive from an ethical perspective (Melrose, 2011). Fear of 'alarming' ethics committees or IRBs by classifying research in this way might lead researchers to downplay the risks by not using 'risky' words such as 'sexuality' or 'gangs' in their proposals or not engaging in this type of research at all (Melrose, 2011).

Most 'practice' research at universities and colleges is not undertaken with high-risk groups or on sensitive topics. However, it is common for master's and PhD students, as well as career academics. It is out of the scope of this book to consider in depth the ethical issues raised by each type of vulnerable group or sensitive topic; they are numerous and complex. For example, there have been discussions about the ethics of community research with urban populations and AIDS (Sieber, 2000, pp. 124–139), the deaf community (Mertens et al., 2009), people with dementia (Wilkinson, 2002) and on topics such as sexuality (Perry, Thurston, & Green, 2004; Roberts et al., 2007).

If you are researching with participants or groups who may be vulnerable or on sensitive/risky topics, it is recommended you increase your ethical 'competence' in that specific area. This can be achieved by reading the relevant literature and talking with other researchers working with similar groups or topics. Contacting relevant charities or user groups, as well as the population you want to work with, will also help identify the key ethical issues and potential solutions.

SUMMARY

The classification of 'vulnerable groups' and 'sensitive topics' identifies participants more vulnerable to ethical abuse or where ethical issues are more profound. These designations stem from the ethical mistreatment of many of these populations in the past. Classifying research populations and topics in this way has benefits (e.g. focuses ethical attention on difficult areas) but may also have unintended ethical consequences. It is important to identify whether your own research works with vulnerable groups or sensitive topics, and if so, which specific ethical issues arise as a result.

CASE STUDY: 'CLOSENESS WITH COSTS' – RESEARCHING WITH PEOPLE WITH LEARNING DISABILITIES

Brad rushed towards Mary as soon as she came in the door and hugged her, turning bright-red as he did so. His mum explained he'd been so excited about her visit; he couldn't wait for the next time to 'tell her about my life'.

Close trusting researcher–participant relationship or ethical dilemma? When researching with people with developmental disabilities, it may be both (Atkinson, 2005; Thompson, 2002). An individual with a learning disability or developmental disability, such as Down syndrome, will typically have problems across a range of functions, including learning, comprehension and communication, as well as having difficulty comprehending social norms. One particular ethical issue which may arise in this research scenario is what Atkinson describes as 'closeness with costs'. Many of the techniques use to improve participatory ethnographic research, such as establishing intimacy and rapport, or taking part alongside everyday activities, can lead to a misunderstanding about the nature of the interaction if researching with people with learning disabilities. This may have 'costs' for the participant, in terms of an expectation of continued friendship or more, dependence and/ or a sense of loss when it ends (Thompson, 2002). People with developmental disabilities may be particularly vulnerable as they often prioritize relationships with 'normal' people as a way of managing the stigma towards those with disabilities and, if able, use strategies to 'pass for normal' themselves (Edgerton, 1993). This may translate into not questioning the researcher, agreeing with their demands, or pleasing the interviewer by (over) sharing private information (Thompson, 2002; Tymchuk, 1997). The boundary issues and expectations raised between researchers and researched are not unique to this research area. However, it is particularly acute. External (e.g. supervision, third-party involvement with carers or advocates) or internal (e.g. diary writing) assessment may be an appropriate ethical safeguards. However, much is dependent on the researcher's ability own to ethically manage expectations and emotions in others.

Ethical Dilemma 10: Older adults as a 'vulnerable group'

Rani, a postgraduate, is hoping to do some research with older people at a care home where she works in the evenings and weekends. She has planned to do participant observation of the structured activities people are involved in (e.g. music, days out), as well some individual interviews about attitudes towards them. Some of the residents are partially sighted/blind and most wear hearing aids. Initially she thought it would be a relatively easy way to collect data, with a group of people who she already has good relations and who are likely to agree. She decided to submit an ethics application to the local health-care committee as some of the residents also have issues with consent (e.g. as a result of dementia). However, now she is starting to think it may be better simply to leave these residents out of the study to make it quicker to gain permission from a university committee instead.

1. Why should/shouldn't Rani include the participants with difficulty consenting from an ethical perspective?
2. How might Rani devise a consent procedure appropriate for the residents?
3. What other ethical issues are raised by this study with a 'vulnerable population'?

---

11 The Ethics of Research with Children and Young People

Children or 'minors' constitute a 'vulnerable group' as far as IRBs and ethics committees are concerned. The issues raised by children beings subjects of research, or involved in participation or policy-making, are legal as well as ethical (Grodin & Glantz, 1994). The guidelines and legislation covering research with children/minors differ slightly between countries and states, depending on factors such as the age of majority (legal age of adulthood). 'Children', for the purposes of this chapter, are those under 18 years old, which is the definition given by the UN Convention on the Rights of the Child.

If you are planning on doing research with children or young people, either as part of education training or academic study, it is important to check with your course leader/ethics officer/ IRB or committee administrator on the specific rules that will apply to you. There is also an extensive literature on the ethical issues, within general research methods books (Christensen & Allison, 2008; Grieg, Taylor, & MacKay, 2007), specific publications (Alderson & Morrow, 2003; Farrell, 2005; Leadbetter et al., 2006; Stanley & Sieber, 1992) and codes developed by charities and disciplinary associations (e.g. Save the Children, 2001). Key issues considered in this chapter include (a) the developmental trajectory and implications for research capacity, (b) issues of power in adult–child relationships, and (c) how to ensure informed consent given these limitations.

KEY ETHICAL ISSUES

Does all research with children require full ethics review?

There are different types of social research which can be conducted with children. One is educational research, usually conducted in school settings. This might involve observing children in their school, conducting educational, cognitive or psychological tests, or conducting an experiment/qualitative activity or intervention at either the individual (e.g. taking part in an experiment to demonstrate colour preference), group (e.g. having children take part in a focus group) or school level (e.g. implementing a phonics-based reading scheme and comparing this with other schools). Other types of research include family research (with or without intervention), the sociology of childhood and anthropological research involving extended families as part of communities. Children and young people may also be consulted in their role as 'service users' within medical and social care (Fajerman, Treseder, & Connor, 2004). Recent trends towards participatory research have occurred in this field, as elsewhere (Save the Children, 2001). Participatory research places importance in asking questions about whose interests is served by any particular research project (e.g. will children either directly or indirectly benefit from the proposed research?) This is coupled with an emphasis on children as active participants in the research process itself; conducting researching 'with' rather than 'on' children.

In the US, certain types of research with children may be exempt from IRB review, or at least be at the discretion of a particular board (see Sieber, 2000, p. 112). These include (a) research in educational settings such as schools which involve investigating teaching methods or comparing them and (b) research involving using educational tests if the results are anonymously held and can't be traced back to the child. Similar projects in the UK are often treated with a 'light touch' review. On the other hand, research with under-8's in the US usually has a Level III risk rating, and so goes to full IRB review. Regulations also differ considerably depending on whether the study meets the criteria for 'minimal risk'. Even if full review is not required, committees/boards or internal ethics procedures will usually request project documentation to act as a record of the work and to assess risk level.

What about child protection/safeguarding?

In the UK, all researchers working with children and other vulnerable groups need a Criminal Records Bureau check (http://www.homeoffice.gov.uk/agencies-public-bodies/crb/, accessed 23/08/2012). This is usually organized by the institution.

During a study, sensitive information may be disclosed by children/minors, such as sexual activity, sexually transmitted diseases (STDs), use of illegal drugs, illness status (e.g. HIV) and child abuse/ neglect. This might come about as part of the project itself (e.g. if researching about teenagers' use of alcohol, it may be likely that disclosures relating to other drugs will occur) or it may occur unexpectedly. How to handle disclosure of sensitive material/issues of confidentiality will need to be discussed in any ethics proposal, particularly if the topic is inherently likely to raise such issues (see Hot Topics: PAC (Chapter 8) and Chapter 6). An ethics of care might also indicate providing information to access advice/assistance in these instances (e.g. encouraging a teenager to talk to someone in authority; offering helpline information).

In relation to child abuse or neglect, the legal obligation to disclose differs between countries and states. However, there is always a moral imperative to protect the vulnerable. For this reason, as discussed elsewhere in the book, if you are researching with children, you should identify the 'ethical chain of command' (i.e. the chain of seniority relating to serious ethical matters) in relation to child protection in your organization. This means that if a child protection issue arises as part of your research, you will know who to contact initially (usually the lead researcher or supervisor), and how to progress any concerns further to a relevant professional (e.g. to child protection services). The issue of child protection is also one reason why ethicists tend to agree that offering confidentiality to children always has to be conditional and not absolute (Neill, 2005). A form of words has to be found in the consent process or form, which explains that the research will be confidential except if something is raised that presents a risk to the child.

There may also be other scenarios which appear relating to abuse or neglect, which require ethical discussion, but the significance of this type of a situation is unclear. An example might be participants disclosing a history of sex abuse or violence (e.g. if interviewing carers who used to work in care homes). It can also arise relatively unexpectedly in interviews, for example, when discussing past health and illness or family relationships. Disclosure of past abusive events can be very upsetting for interviewees; there may also be present consequences depending on the situation (e.g. if prosecution was still a possibility; if any abuser is still in contact with other vulnerable individuals). There is no 'right' way to handle these disclosures, but again, having a 'ethical chain of command' with whom to share and discuss potential courses of action is very important.

Issues of development and power

One of the key issues that needs to be considered when devising ethical research with children is their developmental capabilities and trajectories; clearly researching with very young children or babies has different ethical parameters than, say, researching teenagers' social worlds. Morrow and Richards (1996), in an overview of the area, identify three aspects of being a child which have been identified as problematic from a research ethics perspective:

(a) *Vulnerability*. Children are more vulnerable than most adults in several senses. Firstly, they are physically vulnerable in size and cognitive capacities. They are also mentally/emotionally vulnerable as their lack of knowledge and experience means they are dependent on adults. Secondly, they are structurally vulnerable, as they have a lack of social status and power in areas such as economic, political and social arenas. Ethical attention has tended to focus on the first of these rather than the second (Landsdown, 1994, cited in Morrow & Richards, 1996, p. 97).

(b) *Incompetence*. Incompetence has a legal meaning, as a definition of a lack of capacity for decision-making, including the decision to participate in research (see the Hot Topic on Vulnerable Groups for definitions of capacity (Chapter 10)).

Seeing children as incompetent frames them as lacking ability and/or skills. This can lead to a reliance on adults such as researchers to interpret their actions and meanings, or for parents/those in 'loco parentis' to make decisions about their involvement in research.

(c) *Powerlessness*. There is a considerable disparity in power and status between adults and children. Children are characterized in much research as not giving accurate information, or pleasing the interviewer; and this has led to a distrust of children's accounts. Children also live in multiple scenarios in which they are relatively powerless, in relation to their parents, teachers and other authority figures, which may constrain decisions on participation. Furthermore, access to children is often only possible through institutional gatekeepers who control what research may take place. Morrow and Richards claim this powerlessness aspect is the biggest challenge for ethical research with children.

Morrow and Richards go on to argue that the way in which children are characterized determines ethical practices. For example, characterizing them as 'incompetent' in a legal sense can lead to practices such as not asking children directly for consent, but preferring the consent of the legal guardian, or not recognizing the skills and competencies they do have (e.g. ability to reflect on their experiences) so excluding their 'voices' from the data.

Recent approaches characterize children as 'social actors' who have impact and shape their own worlds; the onus is therefore on the researcher to uncover these rather than impose their own (Kehily, 2007). This has ethical implications. Christensen and Prout suggest that researchers should aim to work in 'ethical symmetry' with children (Christensen & Prout, 2002). The starting point for any project should not be to focus on children's essential vulnerability, but to treat children as adults would be treated in research (e.g. with respect, given the opportunity to consent, to participate), whilst remaining sensitive to the context of the particular research scenario. Although many researchers have been enthusiastic advocates of such participatory approaches, for example, seeing their potential to deliver greater inclusivity (e.g. Cocks, 2006), others remain sceptical about whether such approaches really rebalance the power equation for children, pointing to the inherent structure of research which keeps children as the objects of study and as 'participants' rather than true partners (Pole, Mizen, & Bolton, 1999).

Children from additionally vulnerable groups

It is incorrect to refer to children as a homogenous group for the purposes of ethics. Many children are multiply vulnerable, for example, having learning or developmental difficulties, experiencing difficult lives (e.g. drug use, sexual abuse or criminality either themselves or in their families), living in dangerous or difficult circumstances (e.g. being poor or living in a war zone) or being vulnerable in other ways (e.g. being seriously ill). As discussed in Chapter 4 on ethical research design, deciding the composition of your sample is very much an ethical matter. On the one hand, the principle of social justice implies inclusion and a focus on these groups of children, as they are multiply powerless through their vulnerability. On the other hand, it has been pointed out that 'problem children' are often studied more frequently than 'ordinary children', raising issues about representativeness (Morrow & Richards, 1996) and being the object of study (and perhaps pity).

If you are planning to do research with children who are from a vulnerable group, you should be familiar with the ethical literature on both children and with that particular group. Chapter 10 on 'Hot Topics: Vulnerable Groups and Sensitive Topics' offers a starting point for identifying typical ethical 'flashpoints'. For example, working with 'hard to reach' families in which children may be at real risk requires a clear child protection framework to be developed at the start of the project (Gorin, Hooper, Dyson, & Cabral, 2008).

Working with vulnerable groups may require more creative ethical strategies, for example, Swartz reports on the need to 'go deep' and 'give back' as a white researcher researching black youth in the poorer township areas of South Africa (Swartz, 2011). To 'go deep' she built ethical relationships over a long period of time including living in the area, discussing her 'position' (as a white educated religious professional) reflexively with participants, and using multiple methods to see the topic of study (concepts of morality) from the inside out. 'Giving back' referred to flattening the power gradient (e.g. sharing of resources including money), representing the youth (and her difficulties with the language) fairly, and offering 'research-as-intervention' (e.g. offering listening, intervening to help). Thinking through the ethical aspects of design is important. For example, using unusual methods, such as computer-based questionnaires, may mitigate ethical concerns about privacy in relation to research into the experiences of vulnerable children, but raise other issues concerning lack of support for participants (Davies & Morgan, 2005).

Key questions for research design with children

1. Who benefits from the research project? What are the specific risks and benefits to the children involved? (e.g. distress, interest in project, opportunity to speak and be heard)
2. What are the scenarios in which this research will take place (e.g. classroom, on the street)? How do these present issues concerning vulnerability and powerlessness and how will these be tackled?
3. Who are the participants? Are only adults included, or are children's voices also heard? Are any groups of children excluded, and if so, why?

Quick question

At what age should a young person be able to decide for themselves whether to participate in a research study without parental consent?

CHILDREN AND CONSENT

There is a large literature on how to obtain consent from children (e.g. Alderson & Morrow, 2003; David, Edwards, & Aldred, 2001). In the past, 'proxy' consent was sought on behalf of children, such as from a gatekeeper who is in charge (e.g. a head-teacher or teen youth worker) or parent. Current thinking emphasizes that 'real consent' or 'assent' should be sought from the child, as well as permission from those with parental/other authority (British Psychological Society, 2009, p. 9; Homan, 2001). This is in line with respecting the developing capacity for autonomy of children and adolescents (Kuthner & Posada, 2004).

Definitions

Assent refers to a child's affirmative agreement to take part in research. This may not involve signing a form, but rather agreeing to participate by saying yes or by active participation. A lack of objection to the research (e.g. by not saying 'no') should not be taken as assent. Younger children (aged 5–12 years) are typically asked for assent, whereas older children and teenagers (aged 12+ years) are often able to *consent* in standard terms (e.g. read consent forms and have some capacity to consent), although these ages may vary across jurisdictions.

There are also models of '*opt-in*' (*active*) and '*opt-out*' (*passive*) consent used in educational settings or large surveys. Most research is 'opt-in' in which the participants (parents and children) have to actively agree to participate, for example, by returning a reply slip having read the information. However, this relies on parents to send in the slip and for it not to get lost, which can result in a drastically incomplete data-set. In some instances, an 'opt-out' model is used, where everyone participates, except those who themselves or their parents actively opt out (e.g. by sending in a slip saying they do not want to take part). This would have to be strongly justified to any IRB or ethics committee, as clearly the danger of 'opt-out' is that people who haven't consented but don't actively opt-out are included in the data collection. However, a good case can be made in longitudinal research where large portions of missing data each year would render the study less useful.

Who should consent?

Usually, regulations and guidelines recommend that parental agreement is sought if the child is under the legal age for competency. In the UK this is 18 years. In the US the federal age of consent is also 18 years (although there are variations between states in who is considered a minor). Both require that research with children is screened by an IRB/ethics committee and that parents agree to it. By parental agreement, it means consent from the parents, guardians or, sometimes, from those in 'loco parentis' (e.g. a teacher). For particularly risky/sensitive subjects, both parents may need to agree, although for most topics only one parental signature is sought (the other being 'reasonably unavailable').

This individual consent also rests on the prior consent of key gatekeepers in the study scenario. To undertake research in a school, for example, a student or researcher would start by seeking the permission of the head-teacher or school principal, who may in turn consult other members of staff or governors/school board before making a decision about involvement. Once this overall permission had been agreed, individual consent from parents and children can be sought. It is important to note that for more than minimal risk projects, it is parental, rather than educational permission which is needed.

In general, consent is not required for observation where the researcher is not involved in any way. For example, a typical third-year project on an educational degree might involve observation in the classroom. Permission would be needed from the gatekeepers (head-teacher and teacher) before starting observation.

Some researchers have argued that it is important for people in their teens but under the age of majority (or 18 years old) to able to participate in certain types of research without their parents or teachers knowing about it (for a review in the UK, see Williams, 2006). Examples might include research into topics such as under-age sexuality, cheating in exams or drug use. In the UK, ability to understand information and make decisions without parental consent is termed 'Gillick competency'. In the US, these are referred to as 'emancipated' or 'mature' minors. These are teenagers essentially functioning as adults in terms of being able to make decisions about whether to have health care treatments or whether to participate in a study. It has been pointed out that researchers themselves should not be assessing Gillick competency or minors for inclusion themselves to prevent a conflict of interest (Hunter & Pierscionek, 2007).

Parental permission may also be waived for minimal risk research where it is not possible to contact the parents (e.g. children in orphanages) or where asking for parental permission may cause harm (e.g. if children are at risk of abuse or in state/local authority care) (for more details of parental waivers in the US, see Sieber, 2000 p. 114).

If you are planning to design research which precludes permission being obtained from teachers or parents, seek further advice from your ethics representative/IRB/ethics committee who will be looking for a strong justification, watertight consent procedures and compliance with the regulations.

ISSUES WITH CONSENT

A distinction is often drawn between researching existing activities or behaviour and a study which involves children doing new or additional activities. Generally, if the activity is already occurring, such as a lesson, but some evaluation is added to it by a researcher, this is not considered ethically problematic. This stems from the basis that no additional 'harm' is included by participation in the study; it is what the child was doing anyway. However, there is much research which shows that children, as well as adults with impairments, are often highly compliant and wish to please those in authority (see Hot Topics: Vulnerable Groups and Sensitive Topics (Chapter 10)). They may also disclose more than they intended or was required by the study question. On this basis, classroom research can bring into question the voluntariness of assent/consent. Researchers and teachers need to be reflexive about the power that they have in this situation and alert to indications of children's dissent as well as assent. They also need to consider whether parents may feel some pressure to agree to their children's participation, say, if invited by a class teacher who also teaches and marks their children's work. Some researchers have argued that characterizing children and teenagers as 'vulnerable' and not able to consent frames children negatively (Alderson & Morrow, 2003). From this perspective, the onus is on the researcher to design consent procedures that fit with the comprehension and communication styles of the group. This may mean doing prior investigation about what it means to consent/dissent in that particular age group and on that particular topic beforehand.

Asking parents for permission for their children to participate also contains complex ethical issues (Vargas & Montoya, 2009). Firstly, asking for permission for someone else, in this instance, a child, to participate is not the same as asking someone to participate themselves. Parents may need additional information on what participation will involve for both parents and children, in terms of time and any restrictions or possible harms to their child. They may also need time to negotiate or speak with their child about the matter. Vargas and Montoya also point out that cultures vary in the levels of autonomy they afford their child (e.g. in deferring to parental authority, allowing the child's 'voice' to be heard) and the role of the extended family or other community leaders in decision-making relating to the child. They also suggest that the offering of incentives, such as money, can be problematic within poorer families, as can practical issues such as problems with literacy. I concur with this perspective; seeking consent to research with a child (or indeed any family member) should be done in a way that is respectful of the values and culture of that family, and not seek to disturb family dynamics in a negative way if possible.

WHAT TO INCLUDE IN ASSENT/CONSENT PROCEDURES

Assent/consent procedures are a reduced version of what is offered to adults, using age-appropriate language and/or methods.

The key points to cover are the following:

1. To introduce yourself (e.g. 'Hi, Child X, my name is Hannah and I'm trying to learn more about what you all think about playtimes')
2. To state what the task will involve (in a neutral way avoiding words like 'helping me') (e.g. 'I would like to ask you some questions about what you do in your playtimes. I'll record what you say on this machine so I can listen to it later')
3. To ask for participation (e.g. 'is that ok?' or 'do you want to do this?'); if the answer is *no*, then there is no assent to continue with participation

4. Clarify how the child can dissent (e.g. 'if you want to stop at any time or don't want to take part any more, tell me or your teacher')
5. Give an opportunity to ask questions (e.g. 'have you got any questions about taking part?')
6. Consider whether a signature and or written consent is appropriate for older children.

This procedure could be adapted for different ages and levels of comprehension (e.g. visual method such as pictures or cartoons, tape or video recording, oral consent for younger groups, use of written material at the right level of comprehension). For older children, explaining the benefits/harms of participation and the level of confidentiality offered (e.g. confidential except in cases of serious risk of harm) are also appropriate.

Consent from parents/other gatekeepers has to be gained in advance. For older children, it may be easier to include both parental and child consent on the same form. You also need to consider the difficulties: What happens if hardly any children return the consent slip? How many times will you ask? Is it worth holding a parents meeting to outline the project and what it will involve? If the research is taking place through a school, other organization or community group, it is worth consulting with them about the best ways to gain consent.

Key questions for consent with children

1. *Ensuring voluntariness*. Are the children, or their parents, going to feel pressured or find it difficult not to participate in the research and how will this be managed?
2. *Ensuring information and comprehension*. How will information be given? Is it at the right age/level of comprehension? How will decision-making capabilities be judged?
3. *Ensuring assent/consent*. What will the consent procedure involve? How many people, and who needs to consent? (e.g. will parental consent be sought and if not, why not?) How will children express dissent? How will confidentiality, and its limits, be explained?

SUMMARY

This chapter has summarized some of the extensive literature on the ethical issues raised when researching with children. Key issues include: how to ensure informed consent, inclusive sampling, how to assess risks and benefits to children and ensure their protection. Seeking assent or consent from children themselves is now considered, in many circumstances, best practice. Recent participatory approaches have emphasized the ethical dimensions of incorporating children's voices into research. However, in line with Morrow and Richards (1996) it is arguable that the relative powerlessness of children in relation to the contexts they live, work, play and study continues to present as a major ethical challenge when conducting research. Reflexive thinking and discussion with relevant others doing similar work is a necessary part of increasing ethical competency if researching with children.

Ethical Dilemma 11: Researching friendship in the classroom

Kerry has just arrived at the school for an initial visit where she is conducting a research project looking at how 10- and 11-year-olds understand the concept of 'friendship'. She intends to observe the children in the playground, interview the children in pairs (dyads), asking them about their friendships, as well as do a sorting task on their own to clarify their understandings. The teacher welcomed Kerry to the classroom saying that the children had been told all about the research project and they were very excited about taking part. This is an inclusive school, so the class includes two children with special needs, one having Down Syndrome and another with communication difficulties. The teacher suggests they could do another activity instead as 'clearly they can't take part in the study'.

1. Who needs to consent/assent in this project? How should Kerry go about designing consent/assent procedures?
2. Do you think the two children with special needs should be included in the project? Why or why not?
3. What other ethical issues are raised by this project?

---

12 Internet Research and Ethics

The Internet represents a goldmine in terms of generating data for analysis. Interactions through new media (e.g. Skype, forum messaging) also set up novel possibilities for research. However, Internet research also throws up new ethical challenges because of the way it reconfigures the relationship between the researcher and the researched. This has led to considerable debate over ethical practice (e.g. Berry, 2004; Eysenbach & Till, 2001; Johns, Chen, & Hall, 2004; Jones, 1999; King, 1996; Nancarrow, Pallister, & Brace, 2001). This chapter looks at the key issues that arise in the ethics of Internet research, focusing particularly on how assumptions about the nature of the data indicate different ethical pathways concerning norms such as anonymity, confidentiality and privacy. The ethics of dual-role research, where the researcher is both Internet group member and researcher, is also considered.

Quick question

Where do you post online? Would you be happy for your posts to be included in a research analysis? If yes, would you expect the website name and your post to be anonymized (e.g. your user name changed)?

KEY ETHICAL ISSUES

Online research is a very broad term. It covers three basic types of research, following Eysenbach and Wyatt (2001), with the addition of 'multiple methods':

1. *Passive analysis.* In this research scenario, the researcher is not involved, but studies the online discourses, texts and images

produced by others. Examples of this would include cyberethnography, the study of online communities (e.g. Wilson & Peterson, 2002) and analysis of webpage content (e.g. Saukko, Reed, Britten, & Hogarth, 2010). In the main, the data studied is not produced for the purposes of research, but for social networking, to share experiences, out of boredom, to offer services and so on. As such, it is unlikely that the users have considered that it may be used by researchers.

2. *Active analysis.* In this research scenario, the researcher is a participant. Examples would include participating in an online community whilst studying it or asking questions and clarifying issues with participants by email. It also would include delivering an online intervention through a dedicated website, for example, using trained moderators to intervene on suicide prevention websites (Greidanus & Everall, 2010). Eysenbach and Wyatt point out active analysis often involves deception, but it need not if the researcher chooses to identify themselves and the community is happy to cooperate. The researcher is often in a dual-role as online group participant and researcher simultaneously.

3. *Online forms of traditional research: interviews and surveys.* In this research scenario, the researcher uses online or electronic media to conduct relatively standard research methods. Examples include web surveys sent out to electronic lists, or collecting clinical trial input from participants online.

4. *Multiple methods.* Research projects may encompass more than one method, intertwining traditional methods with Internet analysis. For example, Radin analysed the functions of an online support group for breast cancer sufferers and survivors (Radin, 2006). Methodologically, this encompassed face-to-face, telephone and online interviews with the web mistress, participant observation online and in person and interviews with selected participants. It also incorporated server log analysis of the statistics of forum usage, for example, of which were the most popular pages, or how many 'lurkers' there were and at what point they 'delurked'. The complexity of the available data information sources raises the complexity of the ethical issues (e.g. statistical data connected to user usage is not as sensitive as highly personal disclosures relating to the disease, but may still raise privacy issues).

It is unclear whether Internet research necessarily falls under the remit of IRB/ethics committee review. Some projects do meet the criteria for exemption or 'minimal risk' track review in some institutions; others, particularly for active research, are highly unlikely to be exempt. Guidance is offered by the Association of Internet Researchers (AoIR) (see the Appendix) and by individual IRBs/committees. Researchers should check the likely review requirements of their research carefully.

Some of the key ethical issues raised by Internet research are the following:

1. Participant and researcher become relatively or completely 'invisible' in the research transaction. The act of researching can easily be hidden, by 'lurking' or active deception (not announcing one's intention to research). Equally, the cyber-participant may represent themselves in any way they choose. Electronic communication, through email and Skype, may potentially close this 'gap', as can identifying oneself as a researcher or real-life participant. Safety/risk issues may be raised if virtual and real-life identities are merged.

2. King (1996) argued for considering whether groups are 'open' or 'closed' (i.e. have restricted access). However, much of the Internet is now publically visible and/or membership open to anyone with a valid email address. The anonymity of the Internet encourages high levels of personal disclosure in a public space. This raises the issue of whether it is ethically indicated to maintain privacy and confidentiality for cyber-participants who do not appear to be seeking privacy for themselves or whether to respect their creation of a 'public private space'. Similarly, the issue of informed consent is raised; is it either ethically advisable or practical to seek consent from participants to use material already publically visible? If so, from whom and how, given that users may be numerous, have left the site or changed their contact details?

3. Should Internet data be further anonymized beyond the relative anonymity of most user names? Furthermore, what does it mean to offer 'anonymity' when a quote given in a research paper can be typed back into a search engine and the original source (including perhaps identifying details such as an email address or photos) detected in seconds?

4. Some dual-role research (in which one is both a researcher and an Internet group member) may bring a conflict of interests and/or issues of how and when to disclose one's identity.
5. The boundaries of data collection are expanded. For example, cookies can be deposited on the user's computer when they visit a research site, which can be used to profile visitors even if they then choose not to participate. Similarly, server data can be highly informative about which users are viewing which pages, but raise issues of privacy/consent.
6. Many online communities have their own 'culture' with their own netiquette; as in real-life ethnographic research, the question is raised of how these might be studied with minimum intrusiveness but maximum ethical sensitivity.

PRIVATE OR PUBLIC SPACE?

Some approaches to research ethics on the Internet have emphasized the similarity between traditional and Internet research. From this perspective, all online material is produced by a person, who essentially becomes a 'participant' in this research (whether they know this or not) and should be afforded the protection that other participants are in real-life (RL) research. For example, Battles (2010) used data from an Internet message board to investigate discussions regarding the HPV vaccine amongst adolescents. Despite the public nature of the board, she gave full anonymity, changed the names of the users and website and did not use verbatim quotes. She also emailed all participants individually giving them the option of withdrawing from the study, again as one would do in a face-to-face research protocol.

Another perspective emphasizes that online data is also textual data for which human subject ethics may not be appropriate (Kitchin, 2003). This argument highlights the similarities between the Internet and other forms of cultural production, such as print newspapers, for which consent for analysis would not normally be sought. For example, Bassett and O'Riordan point out that websites associated with minority movements do not just offer private support, but also the opportunity for visibility and representation, for example, for lesbian, gay, bisexual and transgender (LGBT) communities (Bassett & O'Riordan, 2002). In their own study of a website for lesbians, they did follow standard norms of creating a website fake name and alternative user names, but felt uncomfortable as this essentially denied the site visibility. They point out that a purely human subject model of ethics fails to acknowledge the complexity and context of much Internet use and may, at times, produce unethical results.

My own position is that some Internet material arguably falls into the category of online publication. Blogs with no limits on access are written as public texts for people to read and encourage interaction. Analysing the public face of many companies, organizations, pressure groups, appreciation societies seems to be relatively ethically straightforward. Similarly, many print newspapers now have online editions, which encourage anonymized comments; analysing these may be more a matter of copyright (as most sites now assert ownership of this content) than ethics.

However, other material on the Internet is more ambiguous in nature and the risk of 'harm' seems more obvious. Research relating to sensitive topics as detailed in Chapter 10 requires sensitive handling, as does research within sites which run as 'semi-private spaces' in which people disclose their emotions and experiences and who may feel 'invaded' or 'betrayed' by unknowingly being observed or analysed, despite perhaps knowing their posts are publically visible. It has been argued that there are benefits to having a dual researcher/site member role as, once acclimatized, it makes it easier to assess the likely impact of being researched on that virtual community (Chen, Hall, & Johns, 2004).

PRACTICAL ADVICE: INFORMED CONSENT AND ANONYMITY

Informed consent

Using Eysenbach and Wyatt's classification, the type of research will determine, to a large extent, the management of informed consent:

Online forms of traditional research: interviews and surveys. Here, consent is relatively straightforward and similar to offline. So, consent could be sought by ticking a box, participation could be assumed to indicate consent (e.g. behavioural consent for an online survey) or in the case of interviews, a consent form sent by email and returned signed.

Active analysis. Here, the research is essentially an intervention, in which the researcher is involved in the production of data. As such, the onus is on the researcher to seek informed consent and avoid deception, for the reasons outlined in Chapter 7. Lurking or hiding on sites for long periods of time, pretending to be someone else, or adopting an alias are all ethically problematic. If there is a strong rationale for deception (e.g. unable to access significant social phenomenon without it), then again, the RL standard of debriefing and giving the participants the right to withdraw (or for you to leave the group/forum) apply. In many cases, researchers start off as a member of a site and then later wish to conduct research. In these situations, early frankness usually pays off both morally and practically (e.g. informing the site owner, creating a thread to discuss the research, attempting to seek individual consent via email/personal messaging).

Passive analysis. This is the trickiest type of research to undertake from an ethical standpoint. As discussed above, the status of the data, and therefore your ethical obligations to it, are unclear. Even if individual consent is not sought, or it is not practical to do so, consent may be needed from the site owner/host. If consent is not sought, then ensuring anonymity (see below) becomes more important.

Anonymity

In many cases, Internet users have already made themselves anonymous by choosing usernames which disguise their identity. However, this is not always the case. The use of usernames to create privacy (as well as online identities) has evolved over time. Many older usernames contain real names which are easily searchable. Usernames also connect to material not relevant to the study, such as photographs. The real-life identity of online users may also be well-known within a specific community. Furthermore, many postings on Internet are not anonymous but are aimed at seeking publicity (e.g. Twitter).

It has been suggested that it is neither practical nor desirable to anonymize participants in web research; people post having carefully chosen their level of anonymity which need not be overridden by ethics conscious researchers. However, I disagree with this. Research 'transplants' material from one place (the place in which the person originally considered their privacy and anonymity) and places it elsewhere. This may potentially create harms, as well as be libellous if the person felt publically misrepresented. This was not massively problematic when, for example, student projects were read by few people and PhD theses/journal articles were available only in a library. However, the technological power of electronic communication means that research, including participant identities, can be (a) spread into much larger audiences and (b) forever linked and searchable. This could be problematic if the research study is on a contentious or sensitive in which the user never agreed to participate. I have personally taken usernames from a study, typed them into Google, found the original identity of the person and viewed photographs of their latest holiday snaps, but less harmless connections can be imagined. The question should therefore be: 'why not anonymize?' and the harms of not anonymizing be realistically considered in the context of that particular study.

ARE THESE NEW ETHICAL QUESTIONS?

Many of the ethical issues presented by Internet research are not new in themselves. Problems around whether and how to obtain consent from participants, the legitimacy of covert research, preserving anonymity, what counts as a 'public space' and so on pre-date the electronic era. However, the Internet introduces a new dynamic between the researcher and the researched, in which neither can be entirely sure of the identity of the other. Changes in the possibilities of information storage also raise new ethical possibilities. Ethical Internet research norms are developing in response to this over time. I have noticed generational differences in attitudes, with younger groups tending to argue that the responsibility for considering all possible uses of data lies with the the person who posts a message or a picture (e.g. that they should consider that anyone can use their data as research data when they comment on a blog or post pictures). They correspondingly see less need for protection in terms of conventional research ethics.

It is also important to note that Internet research does not represent a net loss in terms of ethics. Internet research offers new research possibilities, for example, the opportunity to access previously unheard voices or experiences, as new constellations of individuals and interests are constituted online. Internet-based research may also bring in new groups of participants, such as younger users, who traditionally would constitute a 'hard to reach' group (Battles, 2010). From a social justice perspective, Internet-based research has much to offer in terms of widening participation. The Internet can also be used to serve traditional ethical goals, such as facilitating greater participant input or increase research impact, for example, by sending a report to all participants via email or placing policy recommendations on a study website.

SUMMARY

These questions are designed to help work through the ethical issues raised by Internet-based research:

1. Who created these 'texts' or 'data'?
2. In what context?
3. What were their expectations of privacy or consent? (insofar as you can guess)?
4. Is the topic sensitive or do the participants constitute a 'vulnerable' group?
5. Are there other 'levels' of consent that need to be sought (e.g. website owners, list organizers/moderators)?
6. What are the harms that could arise?
7. How have other researchers negotiated ethics in similar Internet-based projects in your discipline? (i.e. are there social norms or codes that can guide your ethical thinking?)

Also consider the ethical guidelines for Internet research from organizations such as AoIR. There are no hard and fast ethical rules for Internet research, but conventions are emerging which reflect current thinking about how to be ethical in what is a dynamic research environment.

CASE STUDY: RESEARCHING THE INTERNET GROUP OF WHICH YOU ARE A MEMBER (DUAL-ROLE)

Two postgraduate students decided to use their existing membership of online communities to collect data for their theses. Peter was researching consumer brand preferences in relation to cars. He was already a member of an online fan club forum for one type of car and wanted to look at brand identity by analysing discussions over the past two years. However, although most of the group thought this was a great idea when he initially floated it, one member saw it as 'spying on them' and has even suggested that Peter may be from another rival online forum trying to stir up trouble. Peter's supervisor advised him to use the discussions without seeking consent as they were publically available.

Heather was a member of an online support group for younger people who have ME/ chronic fatigue syndrome (CFS). She had been a moderator there for the past couple of years, having CFS herself from the age of 16. When she started her course, she told lots of the members, who she considers her friends, mentioning the possibility that she might use some of the group's online chat as data. They have been highly supportive, seeing it as 'an opportunity to have our say' and 'share our experiences'. However, Heather has started to worry that the group think her research is more about raising awareness and might be sensitive to the type of in-depth sociological analysis she is intending to produce. Anyone can join both Peter and Heather's forums, although they need a login to post.

At first sight, Peter's topic looks the least sensitive. However, he still had to think through how group dynamics might change as a consequence of analysing existing discussions. He decided not to anonymize the name of the forum as it was related to the brand identity he was studying, but did change usernames. Heather took a different approach. She sought permission from the moderators to set up her own thread on the forum solely for people who wanted to participate in her study. She also emailed some participants off-line. She also talked to participants about the purposes of her analysis and presented it for feedback. There is not necessarily a 'one-size fits all' set of guidelines which work for Internet research; for this reason, both students included ethical reflections in their final theses.

Ethical dilemma 12: Covert research on the Internet

Gina, a PhD student, has decided to research the emergence of sexuality in the early teen years (12–15 years of age). She plans to join social networking sites where this topic is being discussed. Her reason for choosing the Internet is that it is a sensitive but important topic where it is hard to attract participants and/or get parental consent in real life; teens may also talk more frankly online if their identities are hidden. Initially she plans to observe discussion, then join in by presenting herself as a 'teen' at first to gain trust and then later tell the group about her research and seek their consent at this point. She does not want to seek parental consent as she argues that many teens may not have discussed their sexuality with their parents. She will make the material anonymous, by changing usernames, so as to protect the identity of participants.

1. What are some of the ethical issues raised by this study?
2. Will changing the usernames necessarily protect the identity of the participants?
3. How would you change the design of the study to solve some of the ethical issues it currently raises?

Sample Consent Form and Information Sheet

SAMPLE CONSENT FORM

[This could be printed on headed paper from your institution or plain paper with contact details]

Details of study: [include title, name of investigator, name of institution]

☐   I have read and understood the information sheet and had the opportunity to ask questions

☐   I understand that my data will be kept confidential (only shared with the research team) and kept in accordance with data protection legislation

☐   I understand that my name will not be used in any outputs (publications, reports) [also: 'but we will refer to the group of which you are a member/use your job title' or 'how would you like to be identified in any outputs?_____']

☐   I understand I can withdraw from the study at any time, without giving a reason

☐   [Optional: I agree to assign the copyright of my interview data to [name of the researcher] and that it will be stored in a data archive for future use, with identifying details removed]

Name of Participant _____   Signature of Participant _____

Name of Researcher _____   Signature of Researcher _____

Date _____ [Make two copies, one to be retained by the participant, one by the researcher]

SAMPLE INFORMATION SHEET

[I prefer a question and answer format, but you can list the points if you prefer. I have used an interview study on Type 2 diabetes as an example]

[Title of study]

You are invited to take part in the above study. Before you decide whether to participate, please read this information sheet carefully. If you have any questions please call/ask the researcher on the contact details below.

What is the purpose of the study? [short few line description of the purpose of the study]

We are studying how individuals and families think about their risks of getting Type 2 diabetes. We are also interested in what people do, in terms of health behaviour, in relation to this risk. It is hoped that this study will inform better prevention strategies for people who have Type 2 diabetes in their families.

Why have I been invited? [a sentence on sampling]

You have a family member (first-degree relative) with Type 2 diabetes or you have Type 2 diabetes yourself. You are between 18–60 years of age.

What will happen if I take part? [brief description of procedure]

If you decide to take part, researchers [name] or [name] will call you to arrange a convenient time to be interviewed. The interview will take about 1 hour and will be recorded. You will receive a £10 voucher for participating, as well as all travel costs paid (please keep the receipts). We will also ask you if you think any other family members would like to participate.

What are the possible benefits of taking part? [sentence on direct/indirect benefits]

You will get to discuss your experiences of Type 2 diabetes in your family with the interviewer. The results of the study will hopefully feedback to improve clinical care for Type 2 diabetes.

What are the possible risks of taking part? [sentence on risks and further information e.g. helplines or additional sources of support]

Some people may find that thinking about diabetes worries them. Please ask your doctor if you have any questions or worries in relation to Type 2 diabetes. [optional: 'it will not affect your care/involvement in X project in any way if you decide not to participate'].

Confidentiality and data protection [a couple of sentences on how confidentiality/data protection will be ensured, including any limits]

All the information we collect will be treated as confidential and will only be shared with the research team of [me and my supervisor] [optional: except if requested by law/you tell me something that concerns your safety]. We will also make sure that your data is stored securely and anonymously (without your name on it) at the University and then the Data Archive. The audio-files of the interviews will be destroyed five years after the study.

What will happen to the results of the study? [brief details of likely outputs]

Short quotes from your interview will be used in research papers/presentations in a way that will not disclose your identity to others outside the study [For groups: 'You may recognize other family/group members from their interviews and they may recognize you']. The final results of this research will be circulated to doctors and researchers in the UK and elsewhere to help improve prevention.

Who is organizing and funding the study? [also the ethical approval/complaints procedure]

The study is funded by X. The study has been approved by the Social Science Ethics Committee at the University of X. If you have any issues or complaints about the study, please contact [insert name and contact details of authority, such as ethics officer, head of department or for students, your supervisor].

Who do I contact for further information?

If you have questions or want more information on the study, please contact [Your title and name] on [work telephone number] or by email [an institutional one].

Appendix: Ethical Codes, Guidelines and Resources

Any list of ethical codes, guidelines and resources has two issues. One is that new guidelines are issued regularly by key organizations. The other is that any such list cannot be exhaustive. When collecting resources relevant to research ethics, there are several places to look (in addition to this book): (a) your educational institution or organization who will issue guidance relevant to their specific ethics procedures; (b) your disciplinary organization (e.g. American Sociological Association or Oral History Society), which produces guidance relevant for your discipline; and (c) general codes which cross disciplines or focus on specific topics such as data protection or the Internet (e.g. RESPECT code, ESRC guidelines). Some funding is contingent on following given codes (e.g. ESRC/ERC funded projects must follow ESRC/ERC ethical guidelines). This section contains a selection of key codes and guidelines relevant to the social sciences and other disciplines. Date of access for all resources: 23/08/12.

Academy of Management (AoM) (2005). *Code of Ethical Conduct* (www.aomonline.org/governanceandethics/aomrevisedcodeof-ethics.pdf.)

American Anthropological Association. (AAA) (1998). *Code of Ethics of the American Anthropological Association.* (http://www.aaanet.org/committees/ethics/ethcode.htm)

American Anthropological Association (AAA) (2009) *Revisions to Code* (http://www.aaanet.org/issues/policy-advocacy/upload/Ethics-Code-Proposed-Revisions-092208.pdf)

American Evaluation Association (2004). *Guiding Principles and Guiding Principles Training* (http://www.eval.org/Publications/GuidingPrinciples.asp).

American Psychiatric Association (2001, amendments 2009, 2010). *The Principles of Medical Ethics with Annotations Especially*

Applicable to Psychiatry. (http://www.psychiatry.org/practice /ethics/ethics)

American Psychological Association (APA) (2002, 2010 amendments). *Ethical Principles of Psychologists and Code of Conduct* (http://www.apa.org/ethics/code/index.aspx)

Joint Committee on Standards for Educational Evaluation (2011). Program Evaluation Standards, 3rd ed (http://www.jcsee.org /program-evaluation-standards.)

American Sociological Association (ASA) 1999. *Code of Ethics* (http: //www.asanet.org/images/asa/docs/pdf/CodeofEthics.pdf)

American Sociological Association (ASA) (1997). *Policies and Procedures of Committee on Professional Ethics* (http://www.asanet. org/about/ethics/COPE.cfm)

Association of Internet Researchers (http:// www.aoir.org/)

Association of Social Anthropologists (ASA) of the UK and Commonwealth (1999, amended 2011). *Ethical Guidelines for Good Research Practice* (http://www.theasa.org/ethics/guidelines.shtml)

Australian Government, NHMRC (National Health and Medical Research Council) (2007, updated 2009). *National Statement on Ethical Conduct in Human Research* (http://www.nhmrc.gov.au/ guidelines/publications/e72)

Australian Government, NHMRC (National Health and Medical Research Council) (2003). *Values and Ethics: Guidelines for Ethical Conduct in Aboriginal and Torres Strait Islander Health Research* (http://www.nhmrc.gov.au/guidelines/publications/e52)

The Belmont Report (1979). *The National Commission for the Protection of Human Subjects of Biomedical and Behavioural Research. The Belmont Report: Ethical principles and guidelines for the protection of human subjects of research, Department of Health, Education and Welfare, NIH, PHS* (http://www.hhs.gov /ohrp/)

British Psychological Society (BPS) (2009). *Code of Ethics and Conduct* (http://www.bps.org.uk/what-we-do/ethics-standards/ethics-standards)

Also BPS: *Code of Human Research Ethics* (2011) and *Conducting Research on the Internet: Guidelines for Ethical Practice in Psychological Research Online* (2007)

British Sociological Society (2002, updated 2004) *Statement of Ethical Practice* (http://www.britsoc.co.uk/about/equality /statement-of-ethical-practice.aspx)

Canadian Institutes of Health Research, Natural Sciences and Engineering Research Council of Canada and Social Sciences and Humanities Research Council, TCPS-2, *Tri-Council Policy Statement: Ethical Conduct for Research Involving Humans*, December 2010 (http://www.pre.ethics.gc.ca)

ESRC (2010) *Framework for Research Ethics,* Swindon, Economic and Social Research Council (ESRC) (http://www.esrc.ac.uk/_ images/Framework_for_Research_Ethics_tcm8–4586.pdf)

http://www.ethicsguidebook.ac.uk/ (an online guidebook for ESRC researchers and social science in UK)

Health Research Council of New Zealand (2010) *Te Ara Tika: Guidelines for Maori Research Ethics* (http://www.hrc.govt.nz /news-and-publications/publications/maori)

The Missenden Code of Practice for Ethics and Accountability (2002) The Missenden Centre for Higher Education (for UK universities) (http://www.missendencentre.co.uk/docs/MissCode. pdf)

Market Research Society (MRS) Code of Conduct and Guidelines (www.mrs.org.uk/standards/codeconduct.htm)

National Health and Medical Research Council, the Australian Research Council and Universities Australia (2007) *The Australian Code for the Responsible Conduct of Research (*http://www. nhmrc.gov.au/guidelines/publications/r39)

National Institute of Health Bioethics site, US (http://bioethics. od.nih.gov)

National Research Ethics Service for NHS and social care research in the UK (http://www.nres.nhs.uk/). Also search here for the Research Governance Framework.

New Zealand Health and Disability Ethics Committees (includes a list of relevant resources) (http://www.ethics.health.govt.nz)

Office for Human Research Protections (OHRP) covers the regulation of IRBs and research subjects within the US Department of Health and Human Services (HHS) based on the 'Common Rule' Code of Federal Regulations Title 45 (part 46) (http://www.hhs.gov/ohrp).

RESPECT, *An EU Code of Ethics for Socio-Economic Research* (2004) Dench, S. Ifophen, R., & Huws, U. The Institute for Employment Studies. (http://www.respectproject.org/ethics/guidelines.php)

Social Research Association (2003) *Ethical guidelines*. London, SRA (http://www.the-sra.org.uk/documents/pdfs/ethics03.pdf)

World Health Organization, Ethics and Health in Indigenous Peoples (includes sample consent agreements for indigenous peoples) (http://www.who.int/ethics/indigenous_peoples/en/index7.html)

World Medical Association Declaration of Helsinki (most recent 2008): *Ethical Principles for Medical Research Involving Human Subjects* (http://www.wma.net/en/30publications/10policies/b3/)

Bibliography

Adler, P. A., & Adler, P. (2002). Do university lawyers and the police define research values. In W. C. van den Hoonaard (Ed.), *Walking the tightrope: Ethical issue for qualitative researchers* (pp. 34–42). Toronto, Buffalo, London: University of Toronto Press.

Ahmed, A. H., & Nicholson, K. G. (1996). Delays and diversity in the practice of local research ethics committees. *Journal of Medical Ethics*, 22(5), 263–266.

Alderson, P., & Morrow, V. (2003). *Ethics, social research and consulting with children and young people*. Ilford: Barnados.

Allen, L. (2009). 'Caught in the act': Ethics committee review and researching the sexual culture of schools. *Qualitative Research*, 9(4), 395–410.

American Anthropological Association. (1998). *Code of Ethics of the American Anthropological Association*.

American Anthropological Association. (2004). *Statement on Ethnography and Institutional Review Boards*. Retrieved from http://www. aaanet.org/stmts/irb.htm, (Accessed 23/8/12).

American Psychological Association. (2002). Ethical principles of psychologists and code of conduct. *American Psychologist*, 57(12), 1060–1073.

Angell, E., Sutton, A. J., Windridge, K., & Dixon-Woods, M. (2006). Consistency in decision-making by research ethics committees: A controlled comparison. *Journal of Medical Ethics*, 32(11), 662–664.

Annas, G., & Grodin, M. (1992). *The Nazi doctors and the Nuremberg Code*. New York: Oxford University Press.

Association of Internet Researchers. http://www.aoir.org/ (Accessed 23/8/12).

Atkinson, D. (2005). Research as social work: Participatory research in learning disability. *British Journal of Social Work*, 35, 425–434.

Barnes, C., & Mercer, G. (2003). *Disability*. Cambridge, UK: Polity Press.

Bassett, E. H., & O'Riordan, K. (2002). Ethics of Internet research: Contesting the human subjects research model. *Ethics and Information Technology*, 4(3), 233–247.

Battles, H. T. (2010). Exploring ethical and methodological issues in Internet-based research with adolescents. *International Journal of Qualitative Methods*, 9(1), 27–39.

Beauchamp, T. L., & Childress, J. E. (1979). *Principles of biomedical ethics* (1st ed.). Oxford: Oxford University Press.

Beh, H. G. (2002). The role of Institutional Review Boards in protecting human subjects: Are we really ready to fix a broken system? *Law and Psychological Review*, 26 (Spring), 1–47.

Berry, D. (2004). Internet research: Privacy, ethics and alienation: An open source approach. *Internet Research*, *14*(4), 323–332.

Bishop, L. (2005). Protecting respondents and enabling data sharing: Reply to Parry and Mauthner. *Sociology*, *39*(2), 333–336.

Boser, S. (2007). Power, ethics and the IRB: Dissonance over human participant review of participatory research. *Qualitative Inquiry*, *13*(8), 1060–1074.

Boulton, M., & Parker, M. (2007). Introduction: Informed consent in a changing environment. *Social Science and Medicine*, *65*, 2187–2198.

Brabeck, M. M., & Brabeck, K. M. (2009). Feminist perspectives on research ethics. In D. M. Mertens & P. E. Ginsberg (Eds.), *The Handbook of Social Research Ethics* (pp. 39–53). Thousand Oaks, CA: Sage.

Brewer, J. D. (2000). *Ethnography*. Buckingham and Philadelphia: Open University Press.

British Psychological Society. (2009). Code of Ethics and Conduct. Leicester: British Psychological Society.

Brydon-Miller, M. (2010). Covenantal ethics and action research: Exploring a common foundation for social research. In D. M. Mertens & P. E. Ginsberg (Eds.), *The handbook of social research ethics*. Thousand Oaks, CA: Sage.

Bulmer, M. (1982). *Social research ethics: An examination of the merits of covert participant observation* (pp. 1–284). London: Macmillan.

Burbules, N. C. (2009). Privacy and new technologies. In D. M. Mertens & P. E. Ginsberg (Eds.), *The handbook of social research rthics* (pp. 537–549). Thousand Oaks, CA: Sage.

Burgess, M. M. (2007). Proposing modesty for informed consent. *Social Science and Medicine*, *65*, 2284–2295.

Calvey, D. (2008). The art and politics of covert research. *Sociology*, *42*(5), 905–918.

Capron, A. M. (1982). Is consent always necessary in social science research? In T. L. Beauchamp, R. R. Faden, R. J. Wallace, & L. Walters (Eds.), *Ethical issues in social science research* (pp. 215–231). Baltimore, MD: John Hopkins University Press.

Ceci, S. J., & Williams, W. M. (2009). Darwin 200: Should scientists study race and IQ? Yes: the scientific truth must be pursued. *Nature*, *457*, 788–790.

Chen, S. L. S., Hall, G. J., & Johns, M. D. (2004). Research paparazzi in cyberspace: The voices of the researched. In M. D. Johns, S. L. S. Chen, & G. J. Hall (Eds.), *Online Social Research Methods, Issues and Ethics* (pp. 157–175), New York: Peter Lang.

Chomsky, N. et al. (2011, May). Call to reinstate terror academic. *Guardian*. Retrieved from http://www.guardian.co.uk/theguardian/2011/may/10/call-to-reinstate-terror-academci, (Accessed 23/8/12)

Christensen, P., & Allison, J. (2008). *Research with children: Perspectives and practices* (2nd ed.). London: Jessica Kingsley Publishers Ltd.

Christensen, P., & Prout, A. (2002). Working with ethical symmetry in social research with children. *Childhood*, *9*(4), 477–497.

CIHR (2010). Canadian Institutes of Health Research, Natural Sciences and Engineering Research Council of Canada, and Social Sciences and Humanities Research Council of Canada (2010) *Tri-Council Policy Statement: Ethical Conduct for Research Involving Humans*, December 2010.

Clark, T. (2010). On 'being researched': Why do people engage with qualitative research? *Qualitative Research*, *10*(4), 399–419.

Clegg, J. W., & Slife, B. D. (2009). Research ethics in the post-modern context. In D. M. Mertens & P. E. Ginsberg (Eds.), *The handbook of social research ethics* (pp. 23–38). Thousand Oaks, CA: Sage.

Cocks, A. J. (2006). The ethical maze: Finding an inclusive path towards gaining children's agreement to research participation. *Childhood*, *13*(2), 247–266.

Cohen, D. J., & Crabtree, B. F. (2008). Evaluative criteria for qualitative research in health-care: Controversies and recommendations. *Annals of Family Medicine*, *6*(4), 331–339.

Coomber, R. (2002) 'Signing your life away? Why Research Ethics Committees (REC) shouldn't always require written confirmation that participants in research have been informed of the aims of a study and their rights – the case of criminal populations' *Sociological Research Online* Vol. 7, No. 1, http://www.socresonline.org.uk/7/1/coomber.html (accessed 23/08/12)

Coolican, H. (2009). *Research methods and statistics in psychology*. London: Hodder Education.

Corrigan, O. (2003). Empty ethics: the problem with informed consent. *Sociology of Health and Illness*, *25*(7), 768–792.

Corti, L., & Thompson, P. (2003). The secondary analysis of archived qualitative data. In C. Seale, G. Gobo, J. Gubrium, & D. Silverman (Eds.), *Qualitative research practice* (pp. 327–343). London: Sage.

Cutliffe, J., & Ramcharan, P. (2002). Levelling the playing field? Exploring the merits of the ethics-as-process approach for qualitative research proposals. *Qualitative Health Research*, *12*(7), 1000–1010.

Darley, J. M., & Latane, B. (1968). Bystander intervention in emergencies: Diffusion of responsibility. *Journal of Personality and Social Psychology*, *8*, 377–383.

David, M., Edwards, R., & Aldred, P. (2001). Children and school-based research: 'informed consent' or 'educated consent'? *British Educational Research Journal*, *27*(3), 347–365.

Davies, M., & Morgan, A. (2005). Using computer-assisted self-interviewing (CASI) questionnaires to facilitate consultation and participation with vulnerable young people. *Child Abuse Review*, *14*(6), 389–406.

Dench, S., Ifophen, R., & Huws, U. (2004). *RESPECT: An EU Code of Ethics for socio-economic research* (pp. 1–118).

Dingwall, R. (2006). Confronting the anti-democrats: The unethical nature of ethical regulation in social science. *Medical Sociology Online*, *1*, 51–58.

Dixon-Woods, M., Angell, E., Ashcroft, R. E., & Bryman, A. (2007). Written work: The social functions of Research Ethics Committee letters. *Social Science and Medicine*, *65*, 792–802.

Data Protection Act 1998: Guidelines for Social Research (http://www.ico.gov.uk/for_organisations/data_protection/the_guide.aspx, accessed 16/9/2012).

Dreger, A. (2011). Darkness's descent on the American Anthropological Association. *Human Nature*, *22*(3): 225–46.

Edgerton, R. B. (1993). *The cloak of competence*. Revised and updated, California: University of California Press.

Eissenberg, T., Panicker, S., Berenbaum, S., Epley, N., Fendrich, M., Kelso, R., Penner, L., et al. (2004). IRBs and psychological science: Ensuring a collaborative relationship. American Psychological Association. Retrieved from http://www.apa.org/research/responsible/irbs-psych-science.aspx

Ellis, J. (1992). Decisions by and for people with mental retardation: Balancing considerations of autonomy and protection. *Villanova Law Review*, *37*, 1779–1809.

Ennew, J., & Beasley, H. (2006). Participatory methods and approaches: The two tyrannies. In V. Desai & R. Potter (Eds.), *Doing development studies* (pp. 189–199). London: Sage.

ESRC (2010). *Framework for research ethics*. Swindon: ESRC.

Eysenbach, G., & Till, J. E. (2001). Ethical issues in qualitative research on internet communities. *British Medical Journal*, *323*, 1103–1105.

Fajerman, L., Treseder, P., & Connor, J. (2004). *Children are service users too: A guide to consulting children and young people*. London: Save the Children.

Farrell, A. (2005). *Ethical research with children*. Berkshire, England; New York: Open University Press.

Farrimond, H. (2011). Beyond the caveman: Rethinking masculinity in relation to men's help-seeking. *Health*, *16* (2): 208–225.

Farrimond, H., & Kelly, S. E. (2011). Public viewpoints on new prenatal genetic tests. *Public Understanding of Science*. First published on November 15, 2011 as doi:10.1177/0963662511424359.

Farrimond, H., Joffe, H., & Stenner, P. H. D. (2010). A Q-methodological study of smoking identities. *Psychology and Health*, *25*(8), 979–998.

Ferguson, D. (1993). Something a little out of the ordinary: Reflections on becoming an interpretivist researcher in special education. *Remedial and Special Education*, *14*(4), 35–41.

Flick, U. (2006). The quality of qualitative research: Beyond criteria. *An introduction to qualitative research* (3rd ed., pp. 384–397). London: Sage.

Folkman, S. (2000) Privacy and confidentiality. In B. D. Sales and S. Folkman (Eds). *Ethics in research with human participants*. Washington, DC, US: American Psychological Association (pp. 49–57).

Fluehr-Lobban, C. (2002). Globalization of research and international standards of ethics in anthropology. In E. F. Anne-Marie Cantwell & M. Tramm (Eds.), *Ethics and anthropology: Facing future issues in human biology, globalism and cultural property* (pp. 925–937). New York: New York Academy of Sciences.

Gilligan, C. (1982). *In a different voice: Psychological theory and women's development*. Cambridge, MA: Harvard University Press.

Godlee, F., Smith, J., & Marcovitch, H. (2011). Wakefield's article linking MMR vaccine and autism was fraudulent. *British Medical Journal*, *342*, 7454.

Gorin, S., Hooper, C.-A., Dyson, C., & Cabral, C. (2008). Ethical challenges in conducting research with hard to reach families. *Child Abuse Review*, *17*(4), 275–287.

Greenwood, D. J., & Levin, M. (1998). *Introduction to action research: Social research for social change*. London: Sage.

Greidanus, E., & Everall, R. D. (2010). Helper therapy in an online suicide prevention community. *British Journal of Guidance and Counselling*, *38*(2), 191–204.

Grieg, A., Taylor, J., & MacKay, T. (2007). *Doing research with children* (2nd ed.). London, Thousand Oaks, CA: Sage.

Grinyer, A. (2002). The anonymity of research participants: Assumptions, ethics and practicalities. *Social Research Update*, *36*. Retrieved from http://sru.soc.surrey.ac.uk/SRU36.html

Grodin, M., & Glantz, L. H. (1994). *Children as research subjects: Science, ethics and law*. Oxford: Oxford University Press.

Guillemin, M., & Gillam, L. (2004). Ethics, reflexivity, and 'ethically important moments' in research. *Qualitative Inquiry*, *10*(2), 261–280.

Guillemin, M., McDougall, R., & Gillam, L. (2009). Developing 'ethical mindfulness' in continuing professional development in healthcare: use of a personal narrative approach. *Cambridge Quarterly Healthcare Ethics*, *18*(2), 197–208.

HMSO. (2005). *The Mental Capacity Act*. London.

Haggerty, K. D. (2004). Ethics creep: Governing social science research in the name of ethics. *Qualitative Sociology*, *27*(4), 391–414.

Hall, B. L. (1981). Participatory research: Popular knowledge and power, a personal reflection. *Convergance*, *XIV*, 6–17.

Hall, D. (1991). The research imperative and bureaucratic control: The case of clinical research. *Social Science and Medicine*, *32*(3), 333–342.

Halse, C., & Honey, A. (2007). Rethinking ethics review as institutional discourse. *Qualitative Inquiry*, *13*(3), 336–352.

Hammersley, M. (1999). Some reflections on the current state of qualitative research. *Research Intelligence, 70,* 16–18.

Hammersley, M. (2006). Are ethics committees ethical? *Qualitative Researcher,* 2, 4–8.

Hammersley, M., & Atkinson, P. (1995). *Ethnography: Principles in practice.* London: Routledge.

Haslam, S. A., & Reicher, S. (2006). On rethinking the psychology of tyranny: The BBC Prison study. *British Journal of Social Psychology,* 45(1), 55–63.

Hedgecoe, A. (2008a). Research ethics review and the sociological research relationship. *Sociology,* 42(5), 873–886.

Hedgecoe, A. (2008b). A social autopsy of the tgn1412 clinical trial: Northwick park, research ethics committees and the normalisation of deviance. EGENIS seminar series, University of Exeter, Exeter.

Held, V. (2005). *The ethics of care.* Oxford: Oxford University Press.

Hernstein, J. R. & Murray, C. A. (1994). *The bell curve: Intelligence and class structure in American life.* USA: First Free Press.

Herrera, C. D. (1999). Two arguments for 'covert methods' in social research. *British Journal of Sociology,* 50(2), 331–343.

Hinman, L.M. (2008). *Ethics: A pluralistic approach to moral theory,* 4th edn. Belmont, C.A.:Thompson Wadsworth.

Hoffman, V. (1970). Sociological snoopers and journalistic moralizers. *Society,* 7(7), 4–8.

Holloway, W., & Jefferson, W. (2000). *Doing qualitative research differently: Free association, narrative and the interview method.* Thousand Oaks, CA: Sage.

Homan, R. (1991). *The ethics of social research.* London: Longman.

Homan, R. (1992). The ethics of open methods. *British Journal of Sociology,* 1992(43), 321–332.

Homan, R. (2001). The principle of assumed consent: The ethics of gate-keeping. *Journal of Philosophy of Education,* 35(3), 329–343.

Van den Hoonaard, W. C. (2002). Introduction: Ethical norming and qualitative research. In W. C. Van den Hoonaard (Ed.), *Walking the tightrope: Ethical issue for qualitative researchers* (pp. 3–16). Toronto, Buffalo, London: University of Toronto Press.

Humphries, L. (1970). *Tearoom trade: Impersonal sex in public places.* Chicago: Aldine Publishing Company.

Hunt, P. (1981). Settling accounts with the parasite people: A critique of *A Life Apart* by E.J. Miller and G.V. Gwynne. *Disability Challenge,* 1, 37–50.

Hunter, D., & Pierscionek, B. K. (2007). Children, Gillick competency and consent for involvement in research. *Journal of Medical Ethics,* 33(11), 659–662.

Indictment (1949–1953). *Trials of War Criminals before the Nuremberg Military Tribunals under Control Council Law No. 10.* Nuremberg, October 1946–April 1949. Washington, D.C.: U.S. G.P.O.

Jacobsen, N., Gewurtz, R., & Haydon, E. (2007). Ethical review of inter-
pretive research: Problems and solutions. *IRB: Ethics and Human
Research*, 29(5), 1–8.

Johns, M. D., Chen, S. L. S., & Hall, G. J. (2004). *Online social research:
Methods, issues and ethics*. New York: Peter Lang.

Jones, J. H. (1993). *Bad blood: The Tuskegee experiment*. New York:
Free Press.

Jones, S. (1999). *Doing Internet research: Critical issues and methods for
examining the Net*. London: Sage.

Kaufman, S. B., & Wicherts, J. (2011). Black women are not (rated)
less attractive! Our independent analysis of the Add Health dataset.
Beautiful Minds blog, Psychology Today. Retrieved from http://www.
psychologytoday.com/blog/beautiful-minds/201105/black-women-
are-not-rated-less-attractive-our-independent-analysis-the-a (Accessed
23/8/2012).

Kehily, M. (2007). A cultural perspective. In M. Kehily (Ed.), *Understanding youth: Perspectives, identities and practices*. London: Sage in
association with the Open University.

Kellner, F. (2002). Yet another coming crisis? Coping with guidelines from
the Tri-Council. In W. C. Van den Hoonaard (Ed.), *Walking the tightrope: Ethical issue for qualitative researchers* (pp. 26–33). Toronto: University of Toronto Press.

Kelly, S. E., & Farrimond, H. (2012). Non-invasive prenatal genetic testing:
A study of public attitudes. *Public Health Genomics*, 15(2), 73–81.

Kessels, R. P. C. (2003). Patients' memory for medical information. *Journal of the Royal Society of Medicine*, 96(5), 219–222.

Khanlou, N., & Peter, E. (2005). Participatory action research:
Considerations for ethical review. *Social Science and Medicine*, 60,
2333–2340.

Kimmel, A. (1996). *Ethical issues in behavioural research*. Oxford:
Blackwell.

King, S. A. (1996). Researching internet communities: Proposed ethical
guidelines for the reporting of results. *The Information Society*, 12(2),
119–128.

Kitchener, K. S., & Kitchener, R. F. (2009). Social science research ethics:
Historical and philosophical issues. In D. M. Mertens & P. E. Ginsberg
(Eds.), *The handbook of social research ethics* (pp. 5–22). Thousand
Oaks, CA: Sage.

Kitchin, H. A. (2003). The Tri-Council Policy Statement and Research in
Cyberspace: Research Ethics, the Internet, and Revising a 'Living Document'. *Journal of Academic Ethics*, 1(4), 397–418.

Kuthner, T. L., & Posada, M. (2004). Children and adolescents' capacity
to provide informed consent for participation in research. *Advances in
Psychological Research*, 32, 163–173.

LaFolette, M. C. (1994). Fraud in research: Research misconduct. *Society*,
31(3), 6–10.

Latane, B., & Darley, J. (1969). Bystander apathy. *American Scientist*, *57*, 244–268.

Lawton, J. (2001). Gaining and maintaining consent. *Qualitative Health Research*, *11*(5), 693–705.

Leadbetter, B., Banister, E., Benoit, C., Jansson, M., Marshall, A., & Tieckan, T. (2006). *Ethical issues in community-based research with children and youth*. Toronto: University of Toronto Press.

Lenza, M. (2004). Controversies surrounding Laud Humphreys' Tearoom Trade: An unsettling example of politics and power in methodological critiques. *Journal of Sociology and Social Policy*, *24*(3/4/5), 20–31.

Lewin, K. (1946). Action research and minority problems. *Journal of Social Issues*, *2*(4), 34–46.

Lincoln, Y. S., & Tierney, W. E. (2004). Qualitative research and Institutional Review Boards. *Qualitative Inquiry*, *10*(2), 219–234.

Lynn, M., Yosso, T. J., Solorzano, D. G., & Parker, L. (2002). Critical race theory and education: Qualitative research in the new millennium. *Qualitative Inquiry*, *8*(1), 3–6.

Mark, M. M., & Gamble, C. (2009). Experiments, quasi-experiments, and ethics. In D. M. Mertens & P. E. Ginsberg (Eds.), *The handbook of social research ethics* (pp. 198–213). Thousand Oaks, CA: Sage.

Melrose, M. (2011). Regulating social research: Exploring the implications of extending ethical review procedures in social research. *Sociological Research Online*, *16*(2), 14.

Mertens, D. M. (2009). *Transformative research and evaluation*. New York: The Guildford Press.

Mertens, D. M., Holmes, H. M., & Harris, R. L. (2009). Transformative research and ethics. In D. M. Mertens & P. E. Ginsberg (Eds.), *The handbook of social research ethics* (pp. 85–102). Thousand Oaks, CA: Sage.

Miller, T., & Boulton, M. (2007). Changing constructions of informed consent: Qualitative research and complex social worlds. *Social Science and Medicine*, *65*, 2199–2211.

Morrow, V., & Richards, M. (1996). The ethics of social research with children and young people: An overview. *Children and Society*, *10*, 90–106.

Murphy, E., & Dingwall, R. (2007). Informed consent, anticipatory regulation and ethnographic practice. *Social Science and Medicine*, *65*, 2223–2234.

NHMRC. (2007). National Statement on Ethical Conduct in Human Research 2007. NHMRC Publications, Canberra.

Nancarrow, C., Pallister, J., & Brace, I. (2001). A new research medium, new research population and seven deadly sins for Internet researchers. *Qualitative Market Research*, *4*(3), 136–149.

Neill, S. J. (2005). Research with children: A critical review of the guidelines. *Journal of Child Health Care*, *9*(1), 46–58.

Noddings, N. (1984). *Caring: A feminine approach to ethics and moral education*. Berkeley, CA: University of California Press.

Nyambedha, E. O. (2008). Ethical dilemmas of social science research on AIDS and orphanhood in Western Kenya. *Social Science and Medicine, 67*, 771–779.

Oakes, J. M. (2002). Risks and wrongs in social science research: An evaluator's guide to the IRB. *Evaluation Review, 26*(5), 443–79.

Oliver, M. (1992). Changing the social relations of research production? *Disability, Handicap and Society, 7*(2), 101–114.

Palys, T., & Lowman, J. (2002). Anticipating law: Research methods, ethics and the law of priviledge. *Sociological Methodology, 32*, 1–17.

Park, C. (2003). In other (people's) words: Plagiarism by university students – literature and lessons. *Assessment and Evaluation in Higher Education, 28*(5), 471–488.

Parry, O., & Mauthner, N. S. (2004). Whose data are they anyway? Practical, legal and ethical issues in archiving qualitative research data. *Sociology, 38*(1), 139–152.

Patten, M. L. (2002). *Understanding research methods: An overview of the essentials* (3rd ed.). Los Angeles: Pryczak Publishing.

Perry, C., Thurston, M., & Green, K. (2004). Involvement and detachment in researching sexuality: Reflections on the process of semistructured interviewing. *Qualitative Health Research, 14*(1), 135–148.

Pole, C., Mizen, P., & Bolton, A. (1999). Realising children's agency in research: Partners or participants. *International Journal of Social Research Methodology, 20*, 39–54.

Radin, P. (2006). 'To me, it's my life': Medical communication, trust and activism in cyberspace. *Social Science and Medicine, 62*, 591–601.

Ramcharan, P., & Cutliffe, J. (2001). Judging the ethics of qualitative research: Considering the 'ethics-as-process' model. *Health and Social Care in the Community, 9*(6), 358–366.

Redshaw, M. E., Harris, A., & Baum, J. D. (1996). Research ethics committee audit: Differences between committees. *Journal of Medical Ethics, 22*(2), 78–82.

Reicher, S., & Haslam, S. A. (2006). Rethinking the psychology of tyranny: The BBC Prison Study. *British Journal of Social Psychology, 45*(1), 1–40.

Resnick, D. (1998). *The ethics of science*. New York: Routledge.

Roberts, R., Bergstrom, S., & La Rooy, D. (2007). UK students and sex work: Current knowledge and research issues. *Journal of Community and Applied Social Psychology, 17*(2), 141–146.

Rose, S. (2009). Darwin 200: Should scientists study race and IQ? No: Science and society do not benefit. *Nature, 457* (7231), 786–788.

Rosner, F., Bennett, A. J., Cassell, E. J., Farnsworth, P. B., Halpern, A. L., Henry, J. B., Kanick, V., et al. (1991). The ethics of using scientific data obtained by immoral means. *The New York State Journal of Medicine*, *91*(2), 54–59.

Rozovsky, L. E. (1997). *The Canadian law of consent to treatment*. Vancouver: Butterworths.

Saukko, P. M., Reed, M., Britten, N., & Hogarth, S. (2010). Negotiating the boundary between medicine and consumer culture: Online marketing of nutrigenetic tests. *Social Science and Medicine*, *70*(5), 744–753.

Save the Children. (2001). *Children and participation: Research, monitoring and evaluation with children and young people*, Save the Children, London.

Shakespeare, T. (1997). Researching disabled sexuality. In C. Barnes & G. Mercer (Eds.), *Doing disability research* (pp. 177–189). Leeds: The Disability Press.

Shamoo, A., & Resnick, D. (2009). *Responsible conduct of research* (2nd ed.). New York: Oxford University Press.

Shannon, J. (2007). Informed consent: Documenting the intersection of bureaucratic regulation and ethnographic practice. *PoLAR*, *30*, 229–248.

Shweder, R. A. (2004). Tuskagee re-examined. *Spiked*. 8th January, http://www.spiked-online.com/articles/0000000CA34A.htm (Accessed 23/8/12)

Sieber, J. E. (1992). *Planning ethically responsible research: A guide for students and Internal Review Boards*. Applied Social Research Methods Series Volume 31. Newbury Park, London, New Delhi: Sage Publications.

Sieber, J. E. (2000). Planning research: Basic ethical decision-making. In B. D. Sales & S. Folkman (Eds.), *Ethics in research with human participants* (pp. 13–26). Washington, D.C.: American Psychological Association.

Small, R. (2001). Codes are not enough: What philosophy can contribute to the ethics of educational research. *Journal of the Philosophy of Education*, *35*(3), 387–406.

Snyder, L. (2002). Confidentiality and anonymity: Promises and practices. In W. C. van den Hoonaard (Ed.), *Walking the tightrope: Ethical issue for qualitative researchers* (pp. 70–78). Toronto: University of Toronto Press.

Social Research Association. (2003). *Social Research Association Ethical Guidelines* (pp. 1–65). Retrieved from http://www.the-sra.org.uk/documents/pdfs/ethics03.pdf (Accessed: 23/8/2012).

Spicker, P. (2011). Ethical covert research. *Sociology*, *45*(1), 118–133.

Stanley, B., & Sieber, J. (1992). *Social research on children and adolescents: Ethical issues*. Newbury Park, CA: Sage.

Stark, L. (2011). *Behind closed doors: IRB's and the making of ethical research*. Chicago: University of Chicago Press.

Stark, L., & Hedgecoe, A. (2010). A practical guide to research ethics. In I. Bourgeault, R. Dingwall, & R. de Vries (Eds.), *The Sage handbook of qualitative methods in health research* (pp. 589–607). Washington, D.C.: Sage.

Sullivan, M. (2009). Philosophy, ethics and the disability community. In D. M. Mertens & P. E. Ginsberg (Eds.), *The handbook of social research ethics* (pp. 69–84). Thousand Oaks, CA: Sage.

Swartz, S. (2011). 'Going deep' and 'giving back': Strategies for exceeding ethical expectations when researching amongst vulnerable youth. *Qualitative Research*, 11(1), 47–68.

The National Commission for the Protection of Human Subjects of Biomedical and Behavioural Research. (1979). The Belmont Report: Ethical principles and guidelines for the protection of human subjects of research. *OPPR Reports*. Washington, D.C.: Department of Health, Education and Welfare, NIH, PHS.

Thomas, V. G. (2009). Critical race theory: Ethics and dimensions of diversity in research. In D. M. Mertens & P. E. Ginsberg (Eds.), *The handbook of social research ethics* (pp. 54–68). Thousand Oaks, CA: Sage.

Thompson, S. A. (2002). My research friend? My friend the researcher? My friend, my researcher? Mis/informed consent and people with developmental disabilities. In W. C. van den Hoonaard (Ed.), *Walking the tightrope: Ethical issue for qualitative researchers* (pp. 95–106). Toronto: University of Toronto Press.

Tierney, P. (2000). *Darkness in El Dorado: How scientists and journalists devastated the Amazon*. New York: W.W. Norton and Company.

Tymchuk, A. (1997). Informing for consent: Concepts and methods. *Canadian Psychology*, 38(2), 55–75.

Vargas, L. A., & Montoya, M. E. (2009). Involving minors in research: Ethics and law within multicultural settings. In D. M. Mertens & P. E. Ginsberg (Eds.), *The handbook of social research ethics* (pp. 489–506). Thousand Oaks, CA: Sage.

Warren, S. (2002). 'Show me how it feels to work here': Using photography to research organizational aesthetics. *Ephemera: Critical Dialogues on Organizations*, 2(3), 224–245.

White, P. (2009). *Developing research questions: A guide for social scientists*. New York: Palgrave Macmillan.

Wiles, R., Heath, S., Crow, G., & Charles, V. (2005). *Informed consent in social research: A literature review/NCRM Methods Review Paper 001*. Southampton.

Wilkinson, H. (2002). *The perspectives of people with dementia: Research methods and motivations*. Philadelphia, PA: Jessica Kingsley Publishers Ltd.

Williams, B. (2006). Meaningful consent to participate in social research on the part of people under the age of eighteen. *Research Ethics Review*, 2(1), 19–24.

Williamson, G. R., & Prosser, S. (2002). Action research: Politics, ethics and participation. *Journal of Advanced Nursing, 40*(5), 587–593.

Wilson, S. M., & Peterson, L. C. (2002). The anthropology of online communities. *Annual Reviews of Anthropology, 31*, 449–467.

Yin, R. K. (1994). *Case-study research: Design and methods* (2nd ed.). Thousand Oaks, CA: Sage.

Zimbardo, P. G. (1973). On the ethics of intervention in human psychological research: With special reference to the Stanford prison experiment. *Cognition, 2*(2), 243–256.

Zimbardo, P. G. (2006). Commentary: On rethinking the psychology of tyranny: The BBC Prison Study. *The British Journal of Social Psychology, 45*, 47–53.

Zimbardo, P. G., Maslach, C., & Haney, C. (1999). Reflections on the Stanford Prison Experiment: Genesis, transformations, consequences. In T. Blass (Ed.), *Obedience to authority: Current perspectives on the Milgram paradigm* (pp. 193–237). Mahwah, NJ.: Erlbaum.

Ziporyn, T. (1990). What the Nazis called 'medical research' haunts the scientific community to this day. *Journal of the American Medical Association, 263*(6), 791.

Index